# Underground Railroad Tales

## With Routes Through
## the Finger Lakes Region

By Emerson Klees

Illustrated by Dru Wheelin

Friends of the Finger Lakes Publishing

Rochester, New York

Friends of the Finger Lakes Publishing
P. O. Box 18131
Rochester, New York 14618


Library of Congress Catalog Card Number 97-60426

ISBN 0-9635990-8-9

Printed in the United States of America
9 8 7 6 5 4 3 2 1

Cover design by Seneca Mist Graphics, Ithaca, New York
Book design by Dru Wheelin and Terry Ricklefs
Many illustrations are based on photographs by C. S. Kenyon
Maps by Frankly Graphics, Rochester, New York

# Preface

*Underground Railroad Tales With Routes Through the Finger Lakes Region* includes an overview of the slave economy, a brief description of the history of the Underground Railroad, and, divided into four geographic sections, thirty-six tales of the slaves who escaped and the men and women who helped them. These sections are the Midwestern states, the Mid-Atlantic states, the New England states, and the Finger Lakes Region.

The tales relate the hardships faced by the fugitive slaves, who risked danger, separation from loved ones, and punishment to gain their freedom. Yet gain it they did—escaping on foot, by boat, hidden as wagon cargo, and even shipped as rail freight. The stories of the men and women who helped them to escape demonstrate their willingness to expose themselves to injury, imprisonment, and death to aid their fellow men and women.

Biographical sketches of six of the most influential members of the Underground Railroad movement are provided in chapter 5. They are:

- Levi Coffin of Cincinnati, Ohio
- Frederick Douglass of Rochester, New York
- Thomas Garrett of Wilmington, Delaware
- Gerrit Smith of Peterboro, New York
- William Still of Philadelphia, Pennsylvania.
- Harriet Tubman of Auburn, New York

The Finger Lakes Region of New York State was chosen to provide detailed examples of Underground Railroad stations and routes. Chapter 6 provides a description of eight routes through central New York State and forty-one stations, which are supported by maps and illustrations that can be used as guides to locate existing sites on the Underground Railroad.

Many excellent books have been written about the institution of slavery and the Underground Railroad movement. Four of the best are:

- *History of the Underground Railroad* by R. C. Smedley
- *Reminiscences of Levi Coffin* by Levi Coffin
- *The Underground Rail Road* by William Still
- *The Underground Railroad from Slavery to Freedom* by Wilbur H. Siebert

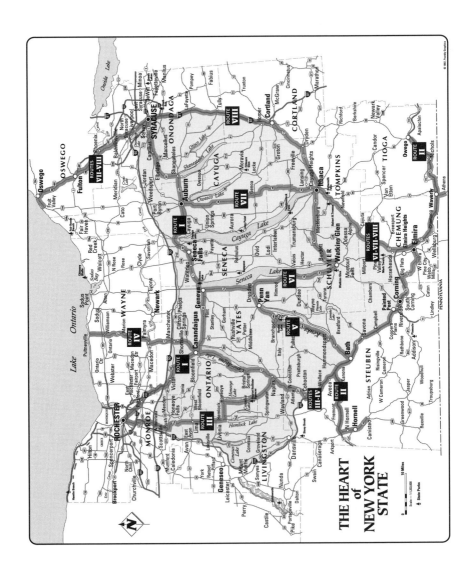

# Table of Contents

# List of Illustrations

Front Cover—Eliza and the Ice Floes Crossing the Ohio River to
Freedom

Back Cover—Slaves Escaping to Smith Creek via a 1,700-foot
tunnel, McGraw, NY

Inside the Book                                              Page No.

# Prologue

## THE SLAVE ECONOMY

*"The whole commerce between master and slave is a perpetual exercise of the most boisterous passions, the most unremitting despotism on the one part, and degrading submissions on the other."*

*Thomas Jefferson*

Slavery was neither new in the eighteenth century nor unique to the United States. Egyptians, Greeks, and Romans are examples of early societies that embraced the institution of slavery. Slavery on a significant scale began in the 1600s when Portuguese ships arrived in Africa, and their crews found that the African peoples did not have stable governments. The Portuguese justified their slave trade on the basis that the Africans themselves held other Africans as slaves. Furthermore, because the Africans were not Christians, the Portuguese thought that it was not necessary to respect their freedom, and that it was permissible to hold them in bondage.

The development of the plantation economy in the United States was fueled by the use of slaves. Slavery thrived in the southern economy because of:

- the growing of labor-intensive crops, such as cotton, rice, sugar cane, and tobacco
- a shortage of other forms of labor
- a low purchase price and a minimum cost of living for slaves

Thousands of slaves were required to grow the South's labor-intensive crops, which were suitable to the climate and soil of the region but could not be grown in many other areas of the country.

Northern farms also required labor, but they tended to be smaller farms than in the South and had easier access to inexpensive immigrant labor.

Plantation owners in the South had tried the employment of indentured servants earlier. They were white men and women who agreed to work for a contracted length of time, usually seven or ten years. However, they usually left the plantation when their period of indenture was over, and new men and women had to be hired and trained. Some of the indentured servants ran away before their contracted period of time was completed.

The South turned to the importation of African-Americans, both from Africa and those who had migrated earlier to the Caribbean islands. They were used to hard work in the fields and were intimidated by having experienced capture and a grim voyage in a slave ship to a strange land. As the slaves were brought to the South in larger numbers, their price decreased.

The value of slaves was increased by advances in agricultural technology. Eli Whitney's invention of the cotton gin in 1793 increased the efficiency of cleaning raw cotton. The gin cleaned five hundred pounds of cotton a day compared with five pounds a day by hand. As the demand for cotton increased and the price increased, more land was cultivated for the crop, and more slaves were required to pick the larger crops.

In 1807, a law was passed forbidding the importation of slaves from Africa and the Caribbean. Owners began to take measures to prevent slaves from escaping and sought ways to bring them back when they ran away. Of the 11,000,000 people in the South in the first half of the nineteenth century, 350,000 owned slaves. The remainder was 4,000,000 slaves and over 6,500,000 non-slaveholding whites, who were also bound to slavery. The slaves were owned by the wealthy plantation masters, and the poor whites were bound economically to the institution of slavery.

In 1793, the Fugitive Slave Law was passed allowing the owner or hired slave-catchers to seize slaves who had run away to another state and return them to their owner. The fine for hiding a runaway slave was $500. African-Americans had to produce documentation that they were free, otherwise any circuit judge or state magistrate could have them arrested and returned to their owner. If the owner couldn't be determined, advertisements were placed in newspapers.

If no owner came forward, the slaves were sold at a slave auction to pay jail expenses and other costs.

The morality of slavery was publicly debated from the time of its inception in the United States in the 1600s. Richard Baxter, an English immigrant living in the North, cautioned, "Remember that they are of as good a kind as you; that is, they are reasonable creatures as well as you, and born to as much liberty. If their sins have enslaved them to you, yet nature made them your equals." He also warned that: "To go as pirates and catch up poor Negroes or people of another land, that never forfeited life and liberty, and to make them slaves, and sell them, is one of the worst kinds of thievery in the world."

Beginning in the late eighteenth century, states began to pass laws abolishing slavery, including Vermont in 1777, Maine and Massachusetts in 1780, New Hampshire in 1783, Ohio in 1803, and Indiana in 1816. Canada passed antislavery laws as well. Upper Canada (Ontario) passed legislation forbiding the importation of slaves in 1793, and Lower Canada (Quebec) followed in 1800.

Alternatives to slavery were sought. One proposal was the establishment of colonies of slaves, either in the United States or in Africa. Two locations that were suggested in the United States were Louisiana and an unspecified site west of the Allegheny Mountains. In 1787, a proposal was made to establish a colony for freed slaves in Sierra Leone. In 1826, the Centerville Abolition Society in Pennsylvania suggested a district "for such persons of color as are opposed to emigrating to Haiti or Liberia." None of these proposals were carried out on a large scale because of cost and impracticality; however, the American Colonization Society reportedly sent to Africa approximately 12,000 African-Americans, nearly half of whom were voluntarily freed by their masters.

In April 1775, the first abolitionist society was established in Pennsylvania. The Abolition Society suspended operation for a time during the Revolutionary War. It resumed operations in 1784 and in 1787 was renamed the Pennsylvania Society for Promoting the Abolition of Slavery, the Relief of Free Negroes Unlawfully Held in Bondage, and for Improving the Condition of the African Race. The Society's first president was Benjamin Franklin. Its goals were to:
- educate the public with speeches, essays, and pamphlets
- petition the courts for more favorable laws

3

- urge and aid blacks to become self-supporting

In 1831, the New England Anti-Slavery Society was organized by William Lloyd Garrison, editor of the antislavery newspaper, *The Liberator*, and eleven other Bostonians at the African Baptist Church on Beacon Hill. In 1833, the American Anti-Slavery Society was formed in Philadelphia. Including William Still of Philadelphia, three of the sixty-two founders were African-Americans. Also in 1833, Lucretia Mott and Margaretta Forten were active in the establishment of the Female Anti-Slavery Society in Philadelphia.

The goal of these societies was to end slavery, not to aid escaped slaves. The more effective these societies became, the closer they came to dismantling the slave economy in the South. Estimates of the number of slaves who escaped to the North range from 40,000 to 100,000. Since slaves were sold for prices ranging from $700 to $2,000, plantation owners' estimates of their losses ranged from $40,000,000 to $200,000,000.

President Lincoln's signing of the Emancipation Proclamation in 1863 abolished slavery. However, slavery didn't come to an end until General Robert E. Lee surrendered to General Ulysses S. Grant on April 9, 1865, and the Thirteenth Amendment to the Constitution was ratified in December 1865.

\* \* \*

# Introduction

## THE UNDERGROUND RAILROAD

*"But if a fugitive claim your help on this journey, break the law and give it to him.... Feed him, clothe him, harbor him, by day and night, and conceal him from his pursuers and from the officers of the law."*
*Charles Beecher—The Duty of Disobedience to Wicked Laws*

American churches were early and continuing supporters of the anti-slavery movement. Among the most active in helping fugitive slaves were the Society of Friends, or Quakers. In 1688 in Germantown, Pennsylvania, Quakers made one of the earliest position statements on the subject: "There is a saying, that we shall do to all men like as we will be done ourselves; making no difference of what the generation, descent or color they are."

They protested "against the traffic in the bodies of men and the treatment of men as cattles [chattels.]" The Quakers believed in human dignity and equality. They based their objection to slavery on the Bible. Among the references to slavery in the Bible is Deuteronomy 23:15-16: "Thou shalt not deliver unto the master the slave which is escaped from his master unto thee. He shall dwell with thee, even among thee in that place which he shall choose in one of thy gates, where it liketh him best; thou shall not oppress him." Isaiah 58:6 provides another reference: "Is this not the fast that I have chosen, to loose the bonds of wickedness, to undo the heavy burdens to let the oppressed go free, and that ye break every yoke."

The Quakers believed that no man or woman should be owned by another. By 1782, all Quaker-owned slaves had been given their freedom. Because they disagreed with the fugitive slave laws, they began to disobey them peacefully; they provided whatever help to the slaves that they could. In 1804, Quakers in Columbia, Pennsylvania, rescued an escaped slave who was a victim of a slave agent's cruelty. The operation organized by the Quakers to help fugitive slaves eventually became the Underground Railroad.

In 1786, George Washington wrote of a slave owned by Mr. Darby in Alexandria who escaped to Philadelphia, and "whom a society of Quakers in that city, formed for such purposes, have attempted to liberate." Washington also wrote that year of a slave of his who had escaped, and "the gentlemen to whose care I sent him has promised every endeavor to apprehend him, but it is not easy to do this, when there are numbers who would rather facilitate the escape of slaves than apprehend them when runaways." Washington let one of his escaped slaves remain in New Hampshire because he didn't want to "excite a mob or riot, or even uneasy sensations in the minds of well-disposed citizens."

Baptist congregations also established societies to aid the slaves, and Presbyterian churches supported education for slaves. In 1842, the Methodist church organized a network to help escaped slaves, and "safe houses" were established throughout the North. The Congregationalist church was very active in helping fugitive slaves. In 1835, they established a college and a colony for escaped slaves in Oberlin, Ohio. Oberlin became a refuge for runaway slaves.

The scale of the operations of the Underground Railroad expanded considerably beginning about 1830. The origin of the name can be traced to 1831 when a fugitive escaped his pursuers after crossing the Ohio River near Ripley, Ohio. The Honorable Rush Sloan of Sandusky, Ohio, was quoted in *The Firelands Pioneer* in July 1888:

> In the year 1831, a fugitive named Tice Davids came over the line and lived just back of Sandusky. He had come direct from Ripley, Ohio, where he crossed the Ohio River.... When he was running away, his master, a Kentuckian, was in close pursuit and pressing him

so hard that when the Ohio River was reached he had no alternative but to jump in and swim across. It took his master some time to secure a skiff, in which he and his aide followed the swimming fugitive, keeping him in sight until he had landed. Once on shore, however, his master could not find him; and after a long ... search the disappointed slave-master went into Ripley, and when he inquired as to what had become of the slave, said ... he ... "must have gone off on an underground road." The story was repeated with a good deal of amusement, and this incident gave the name to the line. First the "Underground Road," afterwards "Underground Railroad."

Railroad trains powered by steam engines began operating in the United States in 1831. It is likely that the term "Underground Road" became "Underground Railroad" after that time.

Currently, the fact that the Underground Railroad was not a real railroad is not universally understood. The Onondaga County Historical Society in Syracuse received a call one day from a woman who was having her house remodeled. She called to tell them that she had just discovered that her home had been a stop on the Underground Railroad. The woman was asked how she knew that her house had been an Underground Railroad station. She said, "The rails are still in the basement."

The Underground Railroad developed a set of titles for its employees. An "agent" was anyone who worked on the Underground Railroad. The fugitive slaves were temporarily housed in "stations," and the owner of the station was a "station master." Those who accompanied the escaped slaves to the next station were "conductors." The larger Underground Railroad organizations had "managers" or "presidents." Individuals who contributed money for clothing, food, and transportation were called "stockholders."

Many of the Underground Railroad routes went through Illinois, Indiana, Michigan, Ohio, Pennsylvania, New Jersey, and the New England States into Canada. The stations were usually between ten and twenty miles apart. The average distance between stations was twelve miles, which was the distance that healthy slaves could walk or that a wagon could travel overnight. All travel was done at night, except in emergencies.

Hiding places in the stations were diverse. They included: attics, basements, cupolas, fake closets, false walls, large ovens, secret rooms, and hidden tunnels. The wagons in which the slaves were transported also had hidden compartments under false floorboards, and some had trap doors. The slaves were covered with blankets, hay, straw, or vegetables. When walking through a town, escaped slaves were given hoes, rakes, and scythes to carry so that they appeared to be working locally. They turned in their tools when they left town. The same tools were returned to the other end of town to be used by the next group of fugitives.

\* \* \*

## ROUTES THROUGH THE MIDWESTERN STATES

In *The Underground Railroad,* Charles L. Blockson cites a study written by Emma Scott in 1934 about routes through Illinois:

> Illinois had five lines of the Underground Railroad, all leading to Chicago or the Illinois River. One ran direct from Chester; another from Alton; yet another from Quincy through Galesburg, Toulon, and Princeton; one from west of the Illinois River to Peoria and on north to Tazewell and Woodford counties; and the fifth from Sparta to Reno, through Springfield, Delavan, Dillon, Elmgrove, Tremont, Deacon Street, Groveland, Martin, Washington, Metamora, Crow Creek, Magnolia, Work Ford, and Greenville to Chicago.

Indiana had many Underground Railroad routes because of its strategic location between the Ohio River and Lake Michigan. Levi and Catherine Coffin of Newport, later called Fountain City, were leaders in the movement. Fugitives were guided across the Ohio River at Diamond Island near West Franklin in Posey County, across the Wabash River at Webbs Ferry, and along the river to Lake, LaPorte, or Porter Counties near Lake Michigan.

Other runaways crossed the Ohio River near Evansville or near the mouth of the Little Pigeon River and on to Boonville and Lynnville in Warrick County. Additional crossings were between Owensboro, Kentucky, and Rockport, Indiana; at Rockport; and near the mouth of the Indiana River in Harrison County.

Ohio had many heavily traveled escape routes via the Great Lakes to Cleveland or Buffalo and to Canada. Cleveland was an active stop for fugitive slaves who arrived from Ripley or by the Oberlin, Richfield route. When Levi and Catherine Coffin moved from Indiana to Cincinnati, they became the leaders of the Underground Railroad in Ohio. Cincinnati's location across the Ohio River from Covington, Kentucky, made it a popular station on the Underground Railroad. The home of Harriet Beecher Stowe, author of *Uncle Tom's Cabin,* and her husband, Calvin, in Walnut Hills was a frequently used station.

Ashtabula County claimed that no slave was ever recaptured within the borders of the county, and Painesville, Ohio, had a reputation of not yielding slaves to owners or slave-catchers. E. Delorus Pearson, Jr., described Underground Railroad activity in Ohio in his article, "The Underground Railroad in Northwest Ohio:"

> An examination of black communities in the state shows that in every case they were active on the road to freedom. Blacks in Seneca County in northwestern Ohio as early as 1825 were assisting fugitives from the South. In the southeastern portion of the state, Burlington, a small Ohio River town, was an important station, and many of the residents of the town today are descendants of conductors and stationkeepers. The practice of free blacks concealing fugitives evidently persisted regardless of the danger, so they can be called an important link on the Underground Railroad.

Michigan's proximity to Canada made it an obvious choice for Underground Railroad routes. In 1838, with the assistance of Levi Coffin in Cincinnati, the Underground Railroad in Michigan began operation. Windsor, Canada, across the river from Detroit, was the most frequent destination of fugitives traveling through Michigan. Some slaves crossed Michigan on foot, and others traveled by schooner up Lake Michigan to the straits and then down Lake Huron.

Researchers at the Detroit Public Library described a route through Michigan in an April 6, 1970, letter to Charles L. Blockson:

> An established route through Michigan started in Cass County, the main entrance to the state, and went through Cassopolis, Schoolcraft, Climax, Battle Creek, Marshall, Albion, Jackson, and other stations along the route of the Michigan Central Railroad, leading to Detroit or farther north, from which points the slaves could be ferried across the Detroit River into Canada. Grand Rapids was a minor station on the Underground, where some fugitives slaves were harbored in a mission house, which later became St. Luke A.M.E. Zion Church operated by the black community.
>
> The routes from the south appear to have led through Toledo, Ohio, and such Indiana towns as Angola, Goshen, South Bend, and Michigan City. Some fugitives however, were transported by the Great Lakes steamers, which carried them from Chicago, Racine, or Milwaukee to Sarnia.

\* \* \*

## ROUTES THROUGH THE MID-ATLANTIC STATES

Philadelphia was one of the important centers of the Underground Railroad movement. Its location just north of the Mason-Dixon Line and its busy port for ships from Delaware, Maryland, and Virginia made it a natural hub. William Still, the son of escaped slaves, was one of the leaders of the Underground Railroad in Philadelphia. Other hubs in Pennsylvania were Carlisle, Lancaster, Meadville, and Pittsburgh. The Monongahela River flowing toward Pittsburgh from the south was an important escape route, and Erie was a popular stop on the way to Canada across Lake Erie or northward to the Niagara River.

Lucretia Mott, who later was a leader in the Women's Rights

Movement, was a leader of the Underground Railroad in Montgomery County, Pennsylvania. Important Berks County stations were Pine Forge, Reading, and White Bar. Harrisburg was a major stop in adjacent Dauphin County. Bucks County stations included Bensalem, Bristol, Buckingham, Doylestown, Newtown, and New Hope, from which the fugitives traveled to Lambertville, New Jersey. The principal route through Delaware County, Pennsylvania, was the West Chester Pike from Philadelphia to Phoenixville. Chester was on the route from Delaware and the Chesapeake Bay. Other active stations included Manor, Media, Newton Square, and Upper Darby.

Fugitives entered Indiana County, Pennsylvania, via Dixonville and traveled to Clearfield County, near Burnside, and into the Grampian Hills. Another route went north through Snyder County to Potter County where it passed through Coudersport, Niles Hill, Millport, and Ceres on the way to Angelica, New York, and ultimately to Canada via Buffalo. Lycoming County stations included Muncy, Peninsula, and Williamsport. Johnstown in Cambria County, Lewisburg in Union County, and Altoona and Hollidaysburg in Blair County were all on active routes.

An important route across southern New Jesey went from Delaware Bay across Cumberland County through Woodbury and Westville in Gloucester County, Gloucester City and Camden in Camden County, and south from Medford via Mt. Holly. Trenton was a major station on the route from Philadelphia to Staten Island. Another active route from Trenton was overland to Jersey City, Newark, and New York City.

The main route through New Jersey went across the Delaware River to Camden, Mt. Holly, Bordentown, Pennington, Hopewell, Princeton, and New Brunswick, where the slave-catchers had their headquarters. The slave-catchers monitored traffic across the Raritan River into Jersey City.

New York City's location dictated that it would become a hub of Underground Railroad activity. In 1829, Isaac Hopper, a leader of the Philadelphia Underground Railroad, moved to New York City where he joined Arthur and Lewis Tappan in the movement. A principal route north from New York City followed the present Star Route 22 to Nassau and Brainerd in Rensselaer County and north to Hoosick and Bennington, Vermont. Another route through New York was

11

from Troy across the Hudson River to the Adirondack Mountains and to Canada via North Elba.

In western New York, Buffalo was a major center on the underground railroad, receiving fugitives from the east via Rochester and from the south via Jamestown and Dunkirk. St. Catherines, Ontario, was the destination of many of the slaves moving through Buffalo.

\* \* \*

## ROUTES THROUGH THE NEW ENGLAND STATES

Aella Green described some of the Underground Railroad routes through New England in an article in the July 14, 1909, Springfield *Sunday Republican:*

> Fugitives fleeing from slavery in the South and reaching New York and Westchester County were heartened there to resume their journey toward freedom in Canada; and then they fared on through the shore towns to New Haven. From thence two routes of the Underground system extended northward across Connecticut, one of them going through Southington and places north of it, and entering Massachusetts at Southwick and Westfield, the other extending through North Guilford and Meriden to Hartford and Springfield. The two routes came together at Northampton.

Five routes radiated outward from Boston, including one that went southeast to Plymouth and another that went through Medford.

The western portion of the Underground Railroad in Vermont went from Bennington County to Burlington and then to Canada via St. Albans. Pownal and Bennington were the southeastern Vermont stations. Other Vermont stations were Manchester, Rutland, Castleton, and Fair Haven. Fugitives boarded canalboats in White Hall for transportation to Canada.

Escaped slaves entered the eastern part of the Vermont Underground Railroad via Brattleboro and either traveled up the

12

Connecticut River to Montpelier, or through the Green Mountains to Otter Creek, Middlebury, Vergennes, Ferrisburg, Charlotte, and Burlington. A spur of this route came from the Hudson Valley through Bennington and Rutland, joining the eastern trunk at Middlebury.

Canaan and Lyme were two of New Hampshire's active stations on the Underground Railroad. Fugitives traveled up the east side of the Connecticut River beyond Haverhill, and then went northeasterly through Franconia and Littleton. They crossed into Vermont at Lunenburg.

In Maine, Portland was a hub of the Underground Railroad that transported fugitive slaves onward to New Brunswick and to Lower Canada (Quebec). Other active stations in Maine were Augusta and Gardiner.

In 1850, a stricter fugitive slave law was passed. It provided sweeping changes supporting the return of escaped slaves. The components of the law included:

- The identification of a slave could be based only on the word of a slave-catcher without verification of any kind.
- The fugitive slaves could not defend themselves.
- There was no fair legal process, such as trial by jury.
- The fee for the commissioner who decided the case was ten dollars if he ruled for the master, but only five dollars if he freed the slave.
- A federal agent could be fined $1,000 if he obstructed the seizure of a fugitive; the agent was held responsible for the value of a slave who escaped from his custody.
- Anyone helping a slave escape could be fined $1,000 and imprisoned for six months.

The principal impact that this fugitive slave law had on Underground Railroad activities was a dramatic increase in the number of escaped slaves going to Canada, where they could not be seized and returned to their masters. Large numbers of escaped slaves living in the North packed up their belongings and moved to Canada after 1850. Harriet Tubman, who conducted 300 slaves to freedom, moved to St. Catherines, Ontario. She said, "I wouldn't trust Uncle Sam with my people no longer."

Eliza and the Ice Floes

# CHAPTER 1

# Underground Railroad Tales
## of the
## Midwestern States

*"Forty-seven slaves I guided toward the North Star, in violation of the state codes of Virginia and Kentucky. I piloted them through the forests, mostly by night; girls, fair and white, dressed as ladies; men and boys as gentlemen, or servants; men in women's clothes, and women in men's clothes; boys dressed as girls, and girls as boys; on foot, on horseback, in buggies, carriages, common wagons, and in and under loads of hay, straw, old furniture, boxes and bags; crossing the Jordan of the slave, swimming or wading chin deep; or in boats or skiffs, on rafts, and often on a pine log. And I never suffered one to be recaptured."*

*– Calvin Fairbanks*

## ALEXANDER MILTON ROSS' STORY

Dr. Alexander Milton Ross, a Canadian abolitionist, was accompanied to his steamboat by Gerrit Smith of Peterboro, New York, and Lewis Tappan of New York. Ross was traveling to New Orleans to feed back information on escaped slaves to Smith and Tappan, who would notify their Underground Railroad associates north of the Ohio River. Their friends in Ohio would forward the "packages of hardware" (men), and "dry goods" (women) to Canada. Ross' hobby was natural history, particularly ornithology, so he planned to travel through the South using the guise of a naturalist.

Ross' visit to New Orleans served to increase his hatred of slavery. He was astounded to attend church on Sunday and hear the minister from the pulpit refer to slavery as a "wise and benificent institution," and that "the institution of slavery was devised by God for the special benefit of the colored race."

Ross observed slave auctions in New Orleans, and the memory of what he saw remained with him. The sobbing and anguish of slaves separated from their husbands, wives, parents, and children weighed heavily upon him. He wished that he could do more to help them. Slave women were beaten because they refused the demands of their overseers. Ross noted that "the horrid traffic in human beings, many of them whiter and more intelligent than the cruel men who bought and sold them, was, without exception, the most monstrous outrage upon the rights of human beings that could possibly be imagined.... "

From New Orleans, Ross traveled to Vicksburg, where he collected orthinological specimens. He had many conversations with slaves as he studied birds on the plantations. They considered Canada to be so far away that they shouldn't even attempt to reach it. He told them of the Underground Railroad that had been organized to help them to freedom in the North and in Canada. He moved on to Selma, Alabama, and then to Columbus, Mississippi. One of the slaves that Ross met had a cruel master who had branded his initials into his slave's back so that he could be easily identified if he ran away. The slave told Ross that he wanted to escape, and Ross confided in him about his mission in the South.

Ross gave this intelligent slave a compass, a knife, a pistol, and directions for reaching friends across the Ohio River in Evansville,

Indiana, and Cleveland, Ohio. Two evenings later while having dinner at his hotel, the hotel owner approached him with an apprehensive look on his face and said, "The Colonel wishes to speak with you. You had better go out and meet him." Ross left the dining room and was confronted by the Colonel, "That's him. Arrest him." A man walked up to Ross and said, "You are my prisoner."

Ross asked why he was being arrested. The Colonel clenched his fist and called Ross an abolitionist who had persuaded his slave to run away. He said that the last that his slave had been seen was with Ross two days previously. The room was crowded, and most of the crowd were glaring at Ross menacingly. The constable placed a pair of handcuffs on Ross' wrists. Ross looked around the room and asked to be allowed to speak. One of the men present said, "Yes, let's hear what he has to say. He ought to be allowed to speak."

Ross said, "Gentlemen, I am a total stranger here, without friends. I am your prisoner in irons. The Colonel has charged me with violating your laws. Will you act the part of cowards by allowing this man to incite you to commit a murder? Or will you, like brave men, grant the only request I have to make, that is, a fair trial before your magistrates?" Several people spoke in favor of Ross receiving a trial, including the owner of the hotel and his wife. Ross was taken to the local jail and confined in a filthy cell.

A large crowd attended Ross' trial. The Colonel stated his side of the case in a very biased manner. Ross thought that his situation was hopeless. He had no friends in town to stand up for him. The Colonel described how Ross had arrived at his plantation the previous Saturday and had asked for permission to shoot birds. The Colonel told how he had permitted his slave, Joe, to go with Ross, and that Joe hadn't returned and couldn't be found. He said that he was certain that Ross had helped Joe escape and demanded that Ross be prosecuted as a thief. The crowd obviously approved of the Colonel's demands.

Ross' chances for release looked bleak. The Justice asked him if he had anything to say in his defense. Suddenly, a man outside the courtroom cried out, "Here's Joe! Here's Joe!" Joe entered the court room and dropped to his knees in front of the Colonel and begged his forgiveness for leaving the plantation without permission. Joe said that on Saturday night he had visited the plantation where his brother lived, which was eight miles away. He had planned on returning home by Sunday evening, but he had sprained his ankle and could not walk on it until Monday evening when he started home.

Joe traveled all night and was told of Ross' arrest when he reached the plantation. Early that morning, he came into Columbus to free Ross. The Justice ordered the constable to release Ross and apologized to him for any inconvenience that they had caused him. The Colonel was disappointed that his version of justice was not implemented. Ross asked a favor of the Colonel, in return for the discomfort that he had caused him. Ross asked that Joe not be punished, and that he be allowed to give Joe a gift. Ross gave Joe a twenty dollar goldpiece, which could be used in a later attempt to escape. Ross realized that Joe had cut short his escape attempt to help him to get out of jail.

Two years later in the American Hotel in Boston, Ross encountered Joe, who was a waiter in the hotel's dining room. He told of his escape, which began the Sunday evening after Ross' acquittal. Joe's brother joined him in the woods near the Colonel's plantation, where they had hidden enough food for several days of their journey. They walked in creek beds and swamps, when they could, to throw the hounds off their scent.

Joe and his brother reached the Ohio River in seventeen days and rowed across it in a borrowed skiff. They traveled in a northeasterly direction and ultimately reached the Cleveland, Ohio, home of a member of the Underground Railroad about whom Ross had told Joe. The fugitives were provided with food and clothing and rested for a week. They were then sent to Canada, where Joe's brother still lived. Joe had decided to return to the United States and was happily settled in Boston.

\* \* \*

## CALVIN FAIRBANKS' STORY

Calvin Fairbanks was attending Oberlin College when he was told of an escaped slave, Barry, whose wife was still in bondage in the South. Fairbanks volunteered to go to Kentucky to help the slave woman escape. On September 1, 1844, he arrived in Lexington, Kentucky, to assist Barry's wife in escaping. He looked into her circumstances, and it appeared unlikely that he would be successful.

While Fairbanks was in Lexington, he was asked to help another slave family to escape. He hired a carriage to transport Lewis Hayden, Hayden's wife, and their son to Ohio. The next morning, they crossed the Ohio River from Maysville, Kentucky, to Ripley, Ohio. Fairbanks contacted Underground Railroad agents in Ohio who provided transportation for the Hayden family to Canada and safety.

Fairbanks returned the hired carriage to Lexington, where he looked for a way to help Barry's wife to escape. However, the Hayden family's master had been provided with information about their means of escape, and Fairbanks was arrested as he entered the city. He was placed in irons in the city jail, where he slept on the stone floor during his confinement of four months and eighteen days.

The law stipulated that "any person found guilty of aiding a slave ... to escape from his ... master, beyond the limits of the State, shall be punished for each offense by an imprisonment of not less than two, nor more than twenty years." On February 18, 1845, Fairbanks was moved to the penitentiary in Frankfort to begin his fifteen-year sentence. During the summer of 1849, Fairbanks' father took a petition to Frankfort requesting his son's release. On August 23, 1849, the Governor pardoned Fairbanks, who had served almost five years of his sentence.

In the fall of 1851, Fairbanks crossed the Ohio River at Jeffersonville, Indiana, and traveled to Louisville, Kentucky, to help a slave woman, Tamar, escape. He returned with her across the Ohio River in leaky skiff, which he rowed with a board. A reward was offered for their capture, and a man whom Fairbanks had trusted turned them in and collected the reward. On November 9, 1851, Fairbanks was seized in Indiana by Kentucky officials and returned to Louisville. He was brought before the Police Judge in Louisville, and bail was set at $5,000. Unable to raise the necessary bail, he was thrown in jail.

At his trial on February 21, 1852, Fairbanks was sentenced to fifteen years' hard labor at the penitentiary in Frankfort, where he was assigned to preparing and spinning hemp. Hemp dust filled the room in which the prisoners worked, and many of them died of lung diseases. Since the prisoners were not provided with vegetables, Fairbanks ate grass and weeds from the exercise yard. On the first occasion that he was whipped in prison, he received thirty-nine lashes from a rawhide whip on his bare back.

Fairbanks' betrothed, Maudana Tileston, moved from Williamsburg, Massachusetts, to Oxford, Ohio, to be nearer to her fiancé. She provided him with bedding, money, and provisions and did everything that she could to make his imprisonment more comfortable. She visited him often, and wrote to him frequently. She "encompassed him with loving observances," and pleaded unsuccessfully with the Governor of Kentucky for a pardon.

Fairbanks was assigned tasks in prison that he was unable to do, and he was whipped when he failed. He said, "I was bound over a chair and my back bared, then I was flogged with a leather strap on my back. I have often counted sixty blows; never many more, I could not. The strap was used because it inflicted more pain, but did the body less harm than the raw hide, which cuts the flesh. I never had my flesh cut by the strap but once; then little particles were found on the wall fifteen feet away."

In April 1864, Fairbanks was pardoned by Lieutenant Governor Jacob. He returned to Cincinnati, where Levi Coffin and the members of the Underground Railroad didn't recognize him, so changed was his appearance. Maudana Tileston, whose loyalty never waivered during their thirteen-year engagement, and Fairbanks were married in the Congregational Church in Oxford, Ohio, on June 9, 1864. They had a happy marriage and were blessed with a healthy son in the fourth year of their union. On her untimely death in September 1876, Fairbanks described his deep feelings for his loyal partner:

> I have suffered an imprisonment of seventeen years and three months. I have suffered from hunger, cold, sickness, insult, corporal punishment, and discontent. But all these sink away into thin air,

into dim, distant nothingness—I count them all joy for righteousness' sake. But this last calamity, this last stroke of misfortune, which has taken from me my stimulating genius, my dependence, my life power, my bosom friend, broods over me in darkness, numbing all my soul....

\* \* \*

## THE CLOSE CALL WITH THE BLOODHOUNDS

A woman slave in Mississippi, who was poor but whose faith was strong, prayed continually in her small hut to escape from the heavy field work and the overseer's lash. She had heard of Canada, but she was concerned that it was too far away for her to reach. She was told that if she followed the Mississippi River north and then veered east following the North Star, she would be free.

Late one night she gathered a small supply of food, put some clothes in a bundle, and quietly left the slave quarters for the nearby forest. She waded through swamps and made her way through canebrakes. She was more willing to risk exposure, starvation, and the alligators and water moccasins in the swamps than to continue to endure the conditions of slavery. After several days, she could hear the bloodhounds on her trail. She waded in pools and streams to throw the bloodhounds off from her scent, but she had to cross many expanses of dry land.

She heard the bloodhounds getting close and began to pray for God to save her. As the bloodhounds approached her, she stood up, took the last crumbs from her pocket—the only food that she had left—and offered it to the hounds. She was afraid that they would bite and mangle her, but they licked the crumbs out of her hand and ran into the forest. She fell to her knees and thanked God for delivering her. She pledged that if she reached Canada safely, she would devote the remainder her life to His service.

For several months she continued on her journey, living on fruit and green corn. She traveled at night and hid in thickets during the day, occasionally stopping at a slave hut to ask for food. She made rafts of logs or poles tied together with vines or hickory withes and poled or paddled across the rivers and larger streams. On reaching

Illinois, she found conductors on the Underground Railroad who helped her to Detroit and across the Detroit River to Canada.

When she reached Canada and freedom, she fell down and kissed the ground. Nearly delirious with joy, she thanked God for helping her reach her destination safely. She became a conscientious worker in the church and fulfilled the vow that she had made on her journey.

\* \* \*

## THE CRAFTY SLAVE

Jim, a clever slave owned by a Kentucky planter, decided to escape from slavery, but told no one—not even his wife and friends. He intended to escape alone, so he waited for a good opportunity. When it presented itself, he headed for the Ohio River. He knocked on the door of a cabin on the shoreline of the river and asked the African-American who answered his knock how he might cross the river. The man in the doorway had a skiff and offered to take Jim across the river for a small fee.

They crossed the river at night and safely reached the opposite shore near Madison, Indiana. Jim was directed to the home of George DeBaptist, a free African-American who was known to help refugee slaves. Jim knew his value to his master and realized that he would be pursued. DeBaptist had heard from his friends that Jim's master was in Madison making inquiries about him.

Jim was guided through cornfields to the next station on the Underground Railroad and onward until he reached the home of William Beard in Union County, Indiana. He stayed there for several days and then traveled to the Newport, Indiana, home of Levi Coffin, a leader of the Underground Railroad. He stayed a day with Levi and Catherine Coffin, then moved on until he reached Canada, where he stayed for several months.

However, he became restless in Canada. He said:

> Oh, how sweet it was to breathe free air, to feel that
> I had no massa who could whip me or sell me. But I
> was not happy long. I could not enjoy liberty when
> the thoughts of my poor wife and children in slavery

22

would rise up before me. I thought to myself, I have learned the way and found friends all along the road; now I will go back and fetch my wife and children. I'll go to the old massa's plantation, and I'll make believe I'm tired of freedom. I'll tell old massa a story that will please him; then I will go to work hard and watch for a chance to slip away with my wife and children.

Jim returned to his old plantation in Kentucky. His master was surprised one morning to see him walking from the slave quarters as if nothing had happened. Jim walked up to his old master, made a deep bow, and stood before him humbly. Jim was greeted with a series of questions and some harsh names. He replied:

I thought I wanted to be free, massa, so I run away and went to Canada. But I had a hard time there, and soon got tired of taking care of myself. I thought I would rather live with massa again and be a good servant. I found that Canada was no place for [us]; it's too cold, and we can't make any money there. Mean white folks cheat poor [African-Americans] out of their wages when they hire them. I soon got sick of being free, and wished I was back on the old plantation. And those people called abolitionists, that I met with along the way, are a mean set of rascals. They pretend to help [us], but they cheat [us] all they can. They get all the work out of [us] they can, and never pay [us] for it. I tell you, massa, they are mean folks.

Jim's master was pleased to hear his story. He asked him to tell his people and the plantation's neighbors about his experiences. Jim worked hard, obeyed well, and regained his master's confidence. When his master was around, Jim spoke ill of his treatment in the North; when his master wasn't around, Jim told his friends and neighbors how well he had been treated on the Underground Railroad and in Canada. Jim applied himself during the fall and winter on the plantation while planning his second escape.

23

In the spring, Jim escaped with his wife and children and hurried toward the Ohio River. The fourteen members of his party all crossed the Ohio River safely. As on his first trip, they were then moved from one Underground Railroad station to another. Jim's party stayed at the Coffins' home in Newport, Indiana, for several days. The fugitives were hidden in the attic when men passed through town looking for them.

Their pursuers looked northward toward Winchester and Cabin Creek. Coffin and his assistants transported Jim and his companions via Spartanburg, Greenville, and Mercer County, Ohio, to Sandusky, Ohio. From there, they went by ship across Lake Erie to Fort Malden, Ontario.

Several years later, Levi Coffin visited Jim in Canada. Jim was happy in his new environment, liked the people, and was able to earn a good living for himself and his family. He was very appreciative of the effort expended by people of the Underground Railroad and of the risks that they took to help their fellow people. He had no feelings of homesickness in Canada and did not miss his old master and the plantation in Kentucky. Jim hoped that God would forgive him for telling his former master so many lies.

\* \* \*

## Eliza and the Ice Floes

Eliza Harris lived with a fear common to many slaves, that she would be sold by her kind owners to others who would not be as kind and protective. If she were sold, she would probably be separated from her two-year-old daughter, Caroline. She had already buried two of her children and couldn't bear the thought of being separated from her surviving child. Her sense of security was shattered when she overheard her master talking about selling her.

Eliza knew that she was going to have to run away and escape to the North. She did her daily chores and waited patiently for nightfall. When the children and the adults with whom she shared the cabin had fallen asleep, Eliza wrapped the sleeping Caroline in a blanket made out of scraps of wool. She quietly walked out of the door, being careful not to awaken anyone.

Eliza had heard the other slaves talking about the big river that separated the slave state of Kentucky from the free state of Ohio. They talked about swimming across the river or crossing by boat. However, it was wintertime, and the river would be covered with ice. Her thin-soled shoes weren't much protection from the frozen ground as she walked the five miles through the woods to the river.

At daybreak, after walking for over two hours, Eliza reached the bank of the river and was disheartened to see that the ice had broken up. Large chunks of ice were floating downstream. She realized that she would have to wait for the temperature to drop overnight to form new ice before she could attempt to cross. She looked for a shelter from the cold. She had heard that there were some free blacks along the river who helped runaways, but she didn't know how to tell which ones would help.

Boldly, Eliza knocked on the door of the closest cabin, and its door was opened by a gray-haired African-American with a gentle expression on his face. She told the man in the doorway that she and her daughter needed a place to stay until nightfall. The man, George, welcomed Eliza into his one-room cabin and introduced himself and his wife, Rosetta, to her. The total furnishings of the cabin were two chairs, a table, and straw matting on the floor near the fireplace, which contained a blazing fire.

Rosetta invited Eliza to sit next to her and gave her some hot broth. George handed a blanket to Eliza and suggested that she get some sleep. She slept most of the day, and, when she awoke, she saw Rosetta feeding some of the broth to Caroline. Rosetta explained that she had been born free, but that George had been born a slave. She had worked long and hard to save money to buy George's freedom.

George, who had left the cabin while Eliza slept, came in with the news that the slave-catchers were going from cabin to cabin searching for her. Eliza, realizing that she was placing her hosts in danger, gathered Caroline into her arms and hurried out the door toward the river. She saw that the river was no closer to being frozen over than it was the previous night. She also saw people in the distance and realized that she was going to have to take her chances crossing the river on the chunks of ice.

Eliza stepped on the nearest large ice chunk and was relieved to find that it supported her weight. She stepped onto the adjacent piece of ice and found that it was solid too. Then onto a third and a fourth chunk, but eventually the ice began to sink and her ankles were soaked with freezing water. The water reached her knees, and she became very nervous because the opposite shore of the river was still thirty feet away. When the water reached her chest, she placed Caroline in her blanket on top of the next large piece of ice and, holding on to its edge with both hands, began to kick her feet to propel them toward the shore.

When they were only ten feet off the Ohio shore near Ripley, Caroline got wet and began to scream. They were about two feet from safety when a man lifted Caroline off the ice, and Eliza pulled herself out of the water. Her pursuers looked across from the Kentucky side of the river, realizing that Eliza had reached freedom.

The man who had helped them from the river took them to an Underground Railroad station. Ohio and Indiana had countless anti-slavery sympathizers and many Underground Railroad conductors and stations. Eliza and Caroline were given food and dry clothing and were sent on to the next Underground Railroad station, the home of Levi and Catherine Coffin at Newport, Indiana. They stayed with the Coffins for several days and were sent with other fugitives by the Greenville branch of the Underground Railroad to Sandusky, Ohio. From there they crossed Lake Erie into Canada and freedom in Chatham, Ontario.

Eliza's escape was described by Harriet Beecher Stowe in *Uncle Tom's Cabin*, a novel published in March 1852. One million copies were sold in the first year of its publication after it was serialized in the *National Era*. Stowe observed that the novel was "written either from observation, incidents which have occurred in the sphere of my personal knowledge, or in the knowledge of my friends. I shall show the best side of the thing, and something faintly approaching the worst."

\* \* \*

## MARGARET GARNER'S STORY

Not all of the stories of escapes from slavery ended happily with freedom in the North or in Canada. Margaret Garner's story is one of the sad stories. In late January 1856, the Ohio River was frozen over, and a group of seventeen slaves who belonged to different masters in the same area of Kentucky decided to attempt to escape. They traveled to the river at night via horse-drawn sled and reached a point below Covington at daybreak. On reaching the Ohio side of the river, the fugitives crossed the river on foot and divided into small groups.

Simon and his wife, Mary, and their son, Robert, and his wife, Margaret Garner, and their four children walked to the home of the Kite family. Joe Kite, whose freedom from slavery had been purchased by his father, was a native of the neighborhood from which the seventeen runaways had come. The fugitives had to ask directions several times before they found the Kites' home below Mill Creek. Unfortunately, this allowed their pursuers to track them. The rest of their party were more fortunate. They were taken to homes maintained by Underground Railroad conductors, who transported them to freedom in Canada.

Kite, who was anxious for his visitors' safety, visited Levi Coffin to ask for advice on moving the eight fugitives from his home. Coffin told him that they were not safe where they were and suggested that they be moved to a settlement of African-Americans in the western part of Cincinnati. Coffin also offered to make arrangements for them to leave the city that evening. But, shortly after Kite returned home, his house was surrounded by police officers, a posse, and the masters of the runaways.

The doors and windows of the Kite house were barred, and the Kite family and the slaves refused to let anyone enter. The fugitives, who were armed, vowed to die rather than be taken prisoner. Margaret threatened to kill her four children to prevent their return to slavery. The posse battered open a window with a log, and a deputy marshal attempted to enter. He was shot in the arm and backed off from his attempt. The pursuers then battered down the door and forced their way into the house.

Robert fired several shots that wounded one of the officers, but he was overpowered and dragged out of the house. Margaret, seeing that they were going to lose their short-lived freedom, grabbed a butcher knife from the kitchen table and slit the throat of her favorite daughter. She attempted to kill herself and the other three children, but she was overpowered before she could do it. The Kites and the fugitives were arrested and taken to jail.

Margaret's trial, which continued for two weeks, was attended by large crowds. The defendant's attorneys asserted that since Margaret had been allowed earlier to come to Cincinnati as a nurse girl, she had been free since that time. Furthermore, her children, who had been born since then, were also free. Commissioner Pendery agreed with the prosecuting attorneys that her voluntary return to a slave state later had invalidated her freedom. He ruled that the fugitives were slaves at the time of their escape.

Lawyer Jolliffe, one of the defendants' attorneys, requested that warrants issued by the state authorities for the arrest of the defendants on criminal charges—Margaret for murder and the others as accessories to murder—be served immediately. Commissioner Pendery wanted to wait until the defendants were out of his jurisdiction. Jolliffe pushed for the warrants to be served: "for the fugitives have all assured me that they will go 'singing to the gallows' rather than be returned to slavery."

According to the Fugitive Slave Law of 1850, if the fugitives passed from the jurisdiction of the court before the warrants were served, they could be returned to bondage. Even a warrant for murder could not be served if the fugitives were returned to the custody of their owners. The fugitives were indicted for murder and as accessories to murder.

Margaret was a twenty-two-year-old mulatto with bright, penetrating eyes. While in the courtroom, she dressed in calico with a white handkerchief around her neck and a yellow cotton turban around her head. She held a nine-month-old baby in her arms. Her two sons, who were four and six years old, sat restlessly next to her. She attracted considerable attention in the courtroom; however, she sat quietly with her eyes cast downward.

The case stirred the citizens of Cincinnati. The legal issues didn't receive much attention. The slaves' desire for freedom and the lengths to which they would go to achieve it were the principal issues. The emotions that drove the fugitives to a decision to die rather than submit to the degradations of slavery captured the hearts of those who attended the trial.

Commissioner Pendery ruled to send the fugitives back to slavery. He said that the decision did not reflect his sympathies, but rather the law of Kentucky and of the United States with respect to property.

On March 11, 1856, the ship on which they were being returned to the South was involved in an accident. Margaret's chains were removed, but the collison with a ship that came to their assistance threw Margaret into the water. Her baby daughter drowned. Margaret and Robert were sold to Judge Bonham and worked on his plantation at Tennessee Landing, Mississippi. Margaret died of typhoid fever in 1858, without ever gaining her freedom. On her deathbed, she advised Robert not to remarry while still in slavery. She counseled him to live in the hope of freedom, which she was confident would come soon in some way.

\* \* \*

## RICHARD DILLINGHAM'S STORY

Richard Dillingham was a schoolteacher and a member of the Society of Friends in Morrow County, Ohio. In December 1848, while visiting Cincinnati, he was asked to travel to Nashville, Tennessee, to help three slaves escape. The slaves left the city in a carriage driven by a freed slave and accompanied by Dillingham on horseback. An African-American whom Dillingham had told of their escape route betrayed him, and they were apprehended at the bridge crossing the Cumberland River. They were jailed overnight.

The slaves were returned to their master, the carriage driver was set free, and Dillingham was held to be charged for his crime. His bail was set at $7,000, an amount that none of his friends could afford to pay. His cell was twelve feet by fifteen feet, and it was shared with six other prisoners. Dillingham wrote to his betrothed, releasing her from her promise to marry him. However, she not only remained faithful and corresponded with him frequently, she wrote to his jailer asking him to provide whatever comforts that circumstances allowed.

Dillingham's trial was conducted on April 13, 1849. His mother and uncle traveled 750 miles to attend and brought with them a certification of his character signed by friends, influential citizens, and civil servants in Ohio. Dillingham spoke to the jury at the end of the trial. He said, " ... Never before in the whole course of my life have I been charged with a dishonest act.... But gentlemen, I have violated your laws. This offense I did commit; and I now stand before you, to my sorrow and regret, as a criminal. But I was prompted by feelings of humanity."

29

Dillingham received a sentence of three years in the penitentiary, the minimum sentence that was allowed for his offense. He was assigned to hard labor in the rock quarry. His health declined, and he became depressed. At the end of his first year of imprisonment, he was assigned as steward at the penitentiary hospital. During the summer of 1850, a cholera epidemic broke out at the penitentiary and many prisoners died. He dispensed medicine to the prisoners and assisted the sick in any way that he could.

One Sunday morning, Dillingham began to show symptoms of the disease. He died that afternoon. In one of his letters to his fiancée from prison, he wrote:

> The nearer I live to the commandment "Love thy neighbor as thyself," the more enjoyment I have of this life. None can know the enjoyments that flow from feelings of goodwill toward our fellow human beings, both friends and enemies, but those who feel and cultivate them. How true it is that "Man's inhumanity to man makes countless thousands mourn."

> Even in my prison cell I may be happy if I will. For the Christian's consolation cannot be shut out from him by enemies or iron gates. Afflictions are often blessings in disguise, and may serve to help us to a more friendly world, which should be the main object in this.

\* \* \*

## THE SOLDIERS AND THE SLAVE GIRL

Early in the Civil War, an attractive, eighteen-year-old mulatto slave girl was sold for $1,700 to a man who planned to place her in a house of prostitution in Lexington, Kentucky. As soon as she heard of her fate, she fled to the camp of the Twenty-second Wisconsin Volunteers in nearby Nicholasville. The regiment was known as the Abolition Regiment because of their antislavery sentiments and those of their commander, Colonel Utley. The Wisconsin volunteers had been ordered to Nicholasville to counter a threatened raid by the Confederate cavalryman, Kirby Smith.

The young slave girl told the soldiers from Racine her story and asked for their protection. The young soldiers agreed to aid her, even though the law didn't permit Union troops to help fugitives who came within their lines. Her master came to the camp, but the men hid her well; she was not discovered. Colonel Utley, who wanted to ensure her safety, asked for two volunteers to take her to the Cincinnati home of Levi Coffin, leader of the Underground Railroad in Ohio.

The two young soldiers were dressed in civilian clothing, and the slave girl was dressed as a soldier. They covered the girl with a load of hay in a supply wagon and left camp in the middle of the night for their over 100-mile journey. Having been given the password though the Union lines, they encountered no problems enroute and arrived safely in the Queen City. The two soldiers brought the girl into the Coffins' sitting room, where they called Levi Coffin aside and told him their story. To the other people present, the girl appeared to be a mulatto soldier boy. Mrs. Coffin showed the "soldier boy" to a room upstairs and the young woman came downstairs the next morning dressed in women's clothes. Her pleasing appearance, good manners, and friendliness impressed her hosts.

The young woman and the two soldiers stayed with the Coffins for two days to rest from their journey. The young men decided to send her to Racine, Wisconsin, where they had friends and relatives. Coffin and the two escorts took her to the railroad station where they put her on a train to Racine via Chicago. Coffin ushered the young woman, who was well-dressed and wore a heavy veil, to her first-class seat. She looked happy as the three men waved good-bye when the train pulled out of the station to take her to freedom.

She arrived safely in Racine and was cared for by friends of the young soldiers. The two young men had the feeling of satisfaction of helping someone in need. There was risk in what they had done, but they were rewarded by knowing that they had played a part in helping a person escape from bondage.

*   *   *

## TWO GIRLS DISGUISED AS BOYS

Two young girls, eleven-year-old Selena Jackson and her ten-year-old sister Cornelia, escaped from their master in Tennessee and traveled over 200 miles to Cabin Creek, Indiana, by themselves. The North Star was their only guide, and the people of Cabin Creek were amazed that the girls had attempted the journey without an adult to accompany them. They hid in thickets and caves during the day and crossed rivers and waded through swamps at night. The girls were hidden in wagons, stowed away on steamboats, and guided on foot though the countryside. They ate farmyard scraps along the way.

Cabin Creek was a popular stop on the Underground Railroad for escaped slaves traveling to Canada because the town's free blacks and freed slaves helped the fugitives to escape. The two sisters were taken in by Bessie Watkins, who had helped many earlier fugitives. Bessie's son, Dosha, blew on a horn to warn his mother that mounted men were approaching the cabin. However, there was no door or window in the back of the cabin for the girls to use to escape, and she didn't have enough warning to hustle them out of the front door.

The four men on horseback fired two shots as they approached Bessie's cabin; she had no doubts as to their reason for coming. Bessie quickly reached into a drawer for clothing that she had saved for this occasion. Then she went to the front door to confront the four men. One man dismounted from his horse, identified himself as the sheriff, and announced that he had a writ that authorized him to search her cabin for "stolen property." Bessie asked what property had been stolen, and one of the other mounted men answered that two of his slaves had been stolen.

The slave-owner accused Bessie of hiding his two slaves. Bessie, who had two sons, pulled the wide-brimmed hats from her sons' heads, and asked the slave owner if he could tell that they were boys. The crowd of townspeople that had gathered in front of Bessie's cabin laughed at her question. Finally, Bessie allowed the sheriff to search the cabin on the condition that if he found any runaway slaves they be given a fair trial in Winchester.

Cornelia and Selena stood in the middle of the single-room cabin, looking like boys in their baggy shirts, oversized rolled-up pants, and slouch hats. As the sheriff and his men entered the cabin, Bessie's son, Dosha, ushered the two disguised girls out of the front door to mingle with the crowd, which had grown to over 200 people. Dosha and a friend had hidden two horses behind some brush near the cabin.

Dosha and his friend helped Cornelia and Selena onto their horses, and then rode slowly down the road leading out of town while the cabin was being searched. Dosha led the two girls to Levi Coffin's house in Newport, about twenty miles away. Slave-catchers arrived in Newport looking for the girls. Catherine Coffin hid the girls between a feather tick and a straw tick and, allowing a breathing space for them, made up the bed as usual, including a coverlet and pillows. They stayed with the Coffins for several weeks until the slave-owner discontinued his search. Then Cornelia and Selena were transported to Canada via the Greenville and Sandusky route of the Underground Railroad.

* * *

## THE VICE PRESIDENT'S SLAVE

Jackson was a slave owned by Vice President William King, who was elected to office with President Franklin Pierce in 1852. Jackson ran away from his master in Washington, D.C., and settled in Cincinnati, where he worked as a barber. He had lived in Cincinnati for several years when his master sent a slave-catcher after him. The slave-catcher hired several men to help him capture Jackson without a writ. They attacked him in the street as he was going to dinner and dragged him to the Walnut Street wharf.

Jackson called out for help, but most of the merchants in the area had gone to dinner. Policemen, who usually sided with the slave-holders, did not come to his aid. One man who attempted to help him was prevented from doing so when Jackson's abductors brandished weapons. Jackson was taken on the ferry boat to Kentucky, transported to Alabama, and served in slavery for three more years. While in Alabama, he married a light-complexioned Creole from Mobile who could pass as a southern lady.

Jackson, who was small in stature, and his wife devised a plan for him to dress as his wife's maid on a business trip to Baltimore. They boarded a river boat in New Oreans that was bound for Cincinnati. They stayed there at the Dumas House, a hotel run by an African-

American. Jackson contacted Levi Coffin of the Underground Railroad, who visited Jackson at the hotel. The hotel manager introduced Jackson's wife to Coffin in the ladies' parlor, where she explained that she wanted to arrange for her servant's escape.

When Coffin asked whether her servant was a man or a woman, she called for her maid, "Sal," to come into the parlor. Sal came into the room, curtsied gracefully, and stood looking at Coffin, who didn't recognize Jackson disguised as a woman. Mrs. Jackson asked Sal to go into the bedroom and bring out the bundle to show to Coffin, who assumed it was a bundle of papers. Jackson returned dressed in a man's suit and carrying the bundle, which was the female attire that he had used as a disguise. Coffin recognized him immediately and greetly him warmly. They laughed at the successfulness of the ruse.

Coffin pointed out that Jackson was too well known in Cincinnati to stay there. He suggested moving to Cleveland. If slave-catchers pursued him, he could easily board a boat and cross Lake Erie into Canada. Jackson established another successful barber shop in Cleveland. He and his wife lived there without any further trouble from slave-catchers.

*   *   *

# CHAPTER 2

# Underground Railroad Tales
## of the
## Mid-Atlantic States

*"If you come to us, and are hungry, we will feed you; if thirsty, we will give you drink, if naked, we will clothe you; if sick, we will minister to your necessities; if in prison, we will visit you; if you need a hiding place from the face of pursuers, we will provide one that even bloodhounds will not scent out."*

—Credo of the American Anti-Slavery Society

## ESCAPING BY "BORROWING" THE MASTER'S CARRIAGES

On November 1, 1855, Harriet Shephard, a mother of five, decided to take action to prevent her children from experiencing the yoke of slavery as she had. Harriet had never received "kind treatment," and she wanted a different life for her daughters and sons. She didn't have enough money to hire a carriage to transport her and Anna Maria, Edwin, Eliza Jane, John Henry, and Mary Ann from Chestertown, Maryland, to freedom. She knew five other slaves who wanted to accompany her on her flight to freedom in the North.

Harriet boldly loaded her children and friends into her master's two carriages when he was otherwise occupied. She headed down the road to Wilmington where she knew she could get help from Thomas Garrett, a leader of the Underground Railroad. When they arrived, Garrett knew that he must get the runaways out of Wilmington quickly, because the master would have men searching for his missing slaves and carriages.

Garrett sent them to Kennett Square, Pennsylvania, a center of abolitionist and Underground Railroad activity. The refugees attended a meeting at the Long Wood meeting house that evening and stayed overnight in Kennett Square. The next morning they were taken to Downingtown and then on to the Kimberton home of Mr. Lewis, a Quaker who assisted fugitives. Lewis transported them to Philadelphia, where the Vigilance Committee sheltered them.

The committee divided up the group, gave them disguises, and sent them to Canada by train. They were not challenged along the way, and they arrived safely in Canada. Harriet knew that she had broken the law by "borrowing" her master's carriages, but she felt that the crime was justified by the conditions.

\* \* \*

## IN A FREE STATE BUT NOT FREE

In 1855, Colonel John Wheeler, a Virginia planter, was appointed U.S. Minister to Nicaragua. Wheeler sold most of his slaves, but he planned to take his slave, Jane Johnson, and her two young sons with him to his new post. Wheeler had sold Jane's oldest son the previous year, and he had planned to sell the two youngest sons before leaving for Central America. However, he decided that if he took Jane's two sons with him, he wouldn't have to hire Indian boys to maintain the minister's residence.

Jane wanted to escape to the North with her two sons before they could be sold. When she heard that Wheeler was going to New York to board a ship bound for Nicaragua, she began to make her plans. They arrived in Philadelphia too late to catch the two o'clock steamboat to New York, and Wheeler went to the Bloodgood Hotel to pass the time until the next boat. He told Jane to sit on a bench in the lobby with her two sons while he went to dinner. He instructed her not to talk to any African-Americans.

An African-American maid walked by the bench, and Jane told her that she and her sons were slaves and wanted to be free. The woman said, "You poor things," and walked away. Another maid walked up the stairs nearby carrying a stack of towels. Jane called out to her, but she didn't stop. Shortly, the same maid, having delivered the towels, walked by again. Jane said, "Sister, my children and I are slaves and would like to be free." The woman asked Jane how long she would be at the hotel. She said, "until five o'clock, then we're taking the boat to New York." The woman said, "Don't worry. I'm going to help you."

At four o'clock, William Still, the head of Vigilance Committee in Philadelphia, received a note, "Mr. Still–Sir: Please come to Bloodgood's Hotel as soon as possible–three slaves here want liberty. Their master is taking them to New York." Still, who had been born a free man, had worked for the Vigilance Committee for the past eight years helping slaves to freedom. In 1850, the work became more difficult when the passage of the Fugitive Slave Law permitted slave owners to capture escaped slaves and return them to the South. U.S. marshals could imprison those who helped escaping slaves, even in the northern states.

On receiving the message, Still visited Passmore Williamson, secretary of the Philadelphia Anti-Slavery Society, who aided runaway slaves. Still asked Williamson to go the Bloodgood Hotel with him because it would be better to have a white man talk with the slaves' owner. Unfortunately, Williamson had a meeting in Harrisburg and couldn't go with Still. Williamson suggested that Still go to the hotel, obtain the names of the slaves, and telegraph ahead to New York to provide help when they arrived there.

When Still was told at the hotel that Wheeler, Jane, and the boys had just left for the wharf, he heard Williamson say over his shoulder that they had better hurry. Williamson commented that Still needed him more than his clients in Harrisburg did. The two men went to the wharf and saw Wheeler, Jane, and her sons sitting on a bench on the upper deck of the steamboat.

Still and Williamson appproached them, and Williamson told Wheeler that he would like to speak to his servant. Wheeler said that anything he had to say to Jane, he could say to him. Williamson told Jane that he wanted to advise her of her rights and asked her if she wanted to be free. Jane replied that she wanted to be free, but that she belonged to Wheeler. Williamson reminded her that she was in Pennsylvania now and that made her free. Wheeler answered for her that she knew she had a right to leave him, but that she chose not to. Jane contradicted him, "I am not free, but I want freedom.... Always wanted to be free ... but he holds me." Wheeler said, "Well, Jane if you want to be free, I'll give you your freedom. I've been planning to do it for a long time anyway."

However, when Jane attempted to leave the boat with the two men, Wheeler attempted to hold her back. Two African-Americans appeared on the scene to help the boys down the ladder to the lower deck, and Williamson took Wheeler by the collar to allow Jane to pass. Still and Williamson took Jane and her two sons to the home of the abolitionists, James and Lucretia Mott, which was a station on the Underground Railroad. Lucretia was a founder of the Philadelphia Female Anti-Slavery Society and later was a leader in the Women's Rights Movement.

After a three-day stay with the Motts, Lucretia told Jane that her old master was causing trouble. She told her that Wheeler had charged the men who had helped her on the steamboat with assault, kidnapping, and rioting. Lucretia then asked her if she would be willing to testify in court against her master. She reminded Jane that, although she was free according to Pennsylvania law, the Fugitive Slave Law of 1850 authorized all slaves to be returned to their masters even if they were in a free state.

Jane agreed to testify. Four days later, she went to court with Lucretia and one of her Quaker friends. A lawyer told Jane that Wheeler had testified that the accused men kidnapped her against her will and asked her if this was true. Jane replied, "I went away of my own free will. Always wanted to be free. Planned to be free when I came north." The lawyer asked her if she would like to go back with Colonel Wheeler. She said that she would rather die.

Jane returned to the Mott home and several days later was on her way to Canada with her sons. The jury had found the accused men not guilty of the kidnapping and rioting charge. The two African-American men who came to her aid on the boat spent a week in jail for assault and battery. Williamson spent over three months in jail. He was charged with contempt of court for filing an evasive report stating that he did not know where Jane was. When he was released, he continued to help other escaped slaves to freedom.

\* \* \*

## JAMES PENNINGTON'S STORY

James Pennington was born into slavery on the Eastern Shore of Maryland. He worked off the plantation with a stonemason until he was eleven years old, when he returned to help build a blacksmith shop for the plantation. When the blacksmith shop was completed, he was apprenticed to the plantation blacksmith.

One of the incidents that motivated Pennington to escape from slavery was seeing his father whipped for no reason. The master was angry that some of his slaves who had been given permission to visit relatives over the weekend had not returned by the start of work on Monday morning.

The master complained to Pennington's father about their lateness in returning and commented that he had too many slaves and would have to get rid of some of them. Pennington's father said that if he were one too many he would find a purchaser to buy him. Suddenly, the master whipped him twenty times on the back and shoulders. Young James saw his father humbled, and he became determined to leave the environment that condoned such mistreatment.

On another occasion, Pennington was shoeing the master's horse when he stood upright to straighten his back briefly. The horse was large, Pennington was tired, and his back hurt. When Pennington stood up, he happened to catch the eye of his master. His master asked him why he was rolling his eyes at him and went into a rage. He struck Pennington repeatedly with his heavy cane and cursed him, despite that fact that he was a hard worker who did quality work. This incident contributed to destroying Penington's pride in doing a good job.

One Sunday in mid-November, Pennington had seen enough mistreatment and fled from the plantation with a few clothes and and a half loaf of Indian bread. He found shelter the second day under a bridge and ate some sour apples that he had picked along the way. He traveled the turnpike road to Baltimore until he was asked if he had papers showing that he was free. When he acknowledged that he didn't, he was advised to stay off the National Turnpike, where he would be asked for papers frequently.

Although he left the turnpike, Pennington was hailed and asked for his papers. He began to run, but his hailer called out to a friend who jumped out into the road with a knife in his hand and grabbed Pennington by the collar. Two other men joined Pennington's assailants who took him to a nearby tavern. They demanded to know his master, but Penington insisted that he was a freed slave without any papers.

Pennington ran from the men while they were taking him to a neighborhood magistrate. He was almost clear of them when a farmer plowing a field dropped his plow and grabbed him by the collar. They returned to the tavern where they again asked Pennington to whom he belonged. He told them that his master was taking a large gang of slaves to Georgia to be sold when many of them contracted smallpox in Virginia and died. The men were much less interested in him after they heard that. They left him in charge of a young boy, from whom he escaped.

Pennington hid in the thick undergrowth in a forest that had been soaked by a heavy afternoon rain. He traveled through a cornfield after leaving the forest. Several ears of corn were the only food that he had eaten in twenty-four hours. He continued to follow the North Star and, upon inquiring of a elderly woman whether he was in Pennsylvania, found that he had crossed the Mason-Dixon Line.

Pennington asked the woman where he could find work and she directed him to the home of a Quaker three miles down the road. He knocked on the door and heard the welcome words, "Come in and take thy breakfast, and get warm." Pennington stayed with the Quaker family for six months, and they taught him how to write. He was transported to another Quaker family in Chester County, Pennsylvania, where he worked for seven months. This family gave Pennington his first copy of the Bible.

Pennington moved on through Philadelphia to New York and Long Island, where he found employment and lived with the family of an elder of the Presbyterian Church. In the spring of 1829, he attended a Sabbath school. He began to think about the slaves in captivity who didn't enjoy the freedoms that he did. In 1834, he met William Lloyd Garrison and the Tappan brothers who were active in the antislavery movement. By then, he had mastered English and was studying Greek, logic, and rhetoric. Pennington set for himself a goal to become a minister.

In order to continue to prepare himself for the ministry, he accepted a teaching position that paid $200 a year. He could not obtain admission to Yale University, but the University did not object when he stood outside of the doors of the classrooms listening to the professors lecture. After becoming a minister, the fulfilment of his pastoral duties was complicated by the fact that he was not permit-ted to ride the horse-drawn trolleys and buses in New York. He was forced to walk considerable distances in order to discharge his duties.

In 1841, Pennington wrote the first African-American history by a black in the United States, A *Text Book of the Origin and History of the Colored People.* He was still legally a slave when he was honored with a Doctor of Divinity degree by the University of Heidelberg, one of Germany's most distinguished universities. Pennington lived a life of accomplishment. He accepted the fact that his youth as a slave had not been well spent, and he was particularly saddened by the fact that his education had begun so late.

\* \* \*

## JOHN BROWN'S STORY

John Brown ran away from his Georgia plantation so many times that his overseer attached bells and horns to his head. An iron ring with a hinge in the back and a hasp and padlock in front was attached around his neck and second iron ring was fitted around the crown of his head. The two rings were joined together by three iron rods that extended three feet above his head. Bells that were attached to the rods, which he considered horns, rang whenever he moved. The contraption, which weighed about fourteen pounds, was designed to help locate him if he ran away again.

Brown wore the bells and horns for three months, day and night, and could not adequately describe the suffering caused by the device. The weight of the contraption made his head, neck, and shoulders ache, particularly when he stooped to work in the fields. His sleep was disrupted because he could neither lie down nor curl up to rest. The device, which he could not remove, prevented him from stretching out, and he was forced to sleep in a crouching position.

When Brown finally escaped to the North, he was so grateful to be free that he didn't know how to behave. Two young Quaker men took him to their home in Pennsylvania and introduced him to their father as "another of the travelers bound to the North Star." Their father laid one hand on Brown's shoulder, shook the other hand, and welcomed him to their home, which was a station on the Underground Railroad. The young men's father took Brown into the parlor, introduced him to his wife, and invited him to breakfast. First they furnished him with clean linen and a suit of clothes and gave him time to wash up.

Brown felt so out of place and was so dumfounded by the family's kindness that he didn't know what to say. Although he was starving, he refused their offer of food. The young men's mother said, "Come, friend John Brown, thee must eat," and loaded his plate with ham, sausage, and eggs. Their father handed him a large piece of bread and said, "Eat away, and don't thee be afraid. We have plenty more in the house." For half an hour, the family urged Brown to eat, but he couldn't eat a bite.

However, once Brown began to eat, he didn't want to stop. He said, "I ate straight on for an entire hour, quite steady." When he had finished all of the food on the table, they brought him some cold salt beef, which he dug into heartily. The father began to cough and wipe his eyes, and the two sons looked at each other with amazement at the quantity of food being consumed. Their mother attempted to distract his eating by getting him to talk, but Brown told her that he could eat and talk at the same time. Finally, she said, "Friend John

Brown, thee mustn't take it unkindly, but thee mustn't eat any more now. Thou canst have some more in the daytime if you like; but you will make yourself ill, if thou take any more now."

A chapter from the Bible was read after breakfast. Including the reading, Brown and the family spent two hours at the breakfast table. Brown, who had been traveling all night, collapsed into bed after breakfast and slept until mid-afternoon, when he was invited to an early dinner. Brown and the family talked until bedtime. He woke up in the middle of the night and couldn't remember where he was, although he knew that he was safe and happy. He thought that he was having some sort of dream or vision. Finally, he remembered that he was in a free state and was safe. He had an overwhelming feeling of freedom and was very appreciative of the help that he had been given in achieving that freedom.

*   *   *

## MARGARET WARD'S STORY

Margaret Ward, who was born on a slave ship between Africa and Baltimore, worked on a plantation on Maryland's Eastern Shore. Margaret received religious instruction and grew into womanhood with many strong traits, including good moral judgment and a firm will. She was also a capable housekeeper-nurse. At the age of twenty, she married another slave. One day her young master threatened to whip her for "resistance to his will." She told him that she would not submit to him and would not endure a whipping either; she would fight him. In fact, she told him that she would rather die than be whipped, and that one of them would die in the attempt. He decided not to risk it.

However, her young master found another way to punish her. He sold her husband, and she watched him driven off with a large group of slaves bound for the New Orleans slave market. Then he turned her over to the harshest overseer on the plantation and told him to work her to the extent of her endurance. The overseer made her work up until the day that she gave birth, and only gave her a week's rest from hard labor in the fields after the birth of her son.

Furthermore, he wouldn't let her son be cared for by the elderly women slaves, which was usually done, while she worked in the

43

fields. She had to bring Samuel with her to the fields and to attempt to find a shady spot for him. One evening she returned to Samuel and found him exhausted from crying, with a large snake lying across his body. Margaret revived him and resolved to escape to the North. She didn't want her son to be subjected to the same yoke that she was enduring. She left the plantation with Samuel at her breast that same evening, following the North Star.

After she had walked a couple of miles, she heard something behind her. She turned around and saw Watch, the mastiff from the plantation, with whom she had always been friends. She tried to get Watch to return to the plantation, but he remembered his evening visits with her and would not leave. She slept during the day, and at night she approached an elderly slave woman to ask for food. The old woman returned about midnight with a plentiful supply of food, which Margaret shared with Watch.

On the second day of her escape, the overseer came looking for her with an old hound and three pups. He didn't bring his best hound because he thought that it would be easy to recapture a woman traveling with a baby. However, on the third day he let his finest hound loose on Margaret's trail and followed on horseback. About noon, the hound found the place where Margaret had slept the previous night and hurried onward in her direction. The young dogs lost Margaret's scent where she forded streams, but the experienced hound stayed on her trail.

Margaret was resting on a riverbank when she heard Watch begin to whine and to become nervous. Then she heard the baying of the approaching bloodhound. With terror, she envisioned herself being seized and bitten by the large hound. The river was too deep to be forded, but she tied Samuel to her shoulders and waded in as far as she could; she carried a club to defend herself. The bloodhound raced ahead and attempted to jump over Watch to get to Margaret, but Watch closed his massive jaws on the hound's windpipe.

The struggle was a silent one. Watch didn't make any noise and the hound couldn't growl. The struggle was fierce, with the hound trying to gain some sort of grip with her front paws. Watch didn't let go until the hound was motionless. Margaret threw the hound's body into the river and hurried onward. Soon afterward, Margaret found people who helped her make her way to Philadelphia, where the Underground Railroad helped her to travel to New York.

In New York, she began a distinguished career as a nurse. She rented a comfortable home for herself, her son, and Watch, while he lived. Samuel began his education in Westchester County, and then continued it while working for Gerrit Smith in Peterboro, Madison County. Samuel obtained an excellent education and became a minister in the  Congregational Church. He became a member of the Underground Railroad and was an eloquent speaker in the pulpit.

\* \* \*

## "MISTER" MARIA WEEMS

Maria Weems, a fifteen-year-old slave girl, lived with her master and mistress in  Rockville, Maryland. She expressed an interest to friends in Washington, D.C., in escaping to North and became the subject of many letters planning her escape. The letters were written between J. Bigelow of Washington and William Still of Philadelphia, a leader in the Underground Railroad, over a period of two years. They arranged for her to dress in male attire and travel as a lad named "Joe Wright."

After helping her to escape from her master's house, Bigelow arranged for Dr. H's carriage, without a driver, to be standing outside of the White House. Bigelow shook Dr. H's hand and wished him a safe journey as Joe climbed onto the carriage and took the reins. Dr. H gave Joe the directions to Maryland and took the reins himself when they were out of the city. Dr. H had friends in Maryland and decided to stay with them the first night instead of taking a chance on staying at an inn. His friends were pleased to see him and welcomed him to their farmhouse.

The doctor and his friends talked in the parlor until Dr. H said he was feeling a "little languid" and thought he should retire. He told his friends that he was "liable to vertigo" and that it might be better if Joe slept in his room with him. He told them, "Simply give him a bed quilt and he will fare well enough in one corner of the room." Dr. H rose early the next morning and ate a hearty breakfast with his friends. Dr. H thanked his friends for their hospitality, said goodbye to them, and pointed the carriage toward Pennsylvania.

Joe Wright, alias Maria Weems, was a happy young woman that

evening when they crossed the Mason-Dixon line. Dr. H and Maria arrived at William Still's home in Philadelphia on Thanksgiving Day, 1855. Still wasn't home, so Dr. H told Mrs. Still, "I wish to leave this young lad with you a short while, and I will call and see further about him." Dr. H wanted to let his wife know that he had returned safely.

Still and his friends were surprised at how well the disguise worked. In her new suit, Maria deceived everyone who saw her, including the members of the Vigilance Committee. The Underground Railroad transported Maria to the home of Reverend A. N. Freeman in New York and subsequently to Canada, where she was educated at the Buxton Settlement.

* * *

## SETH CONCKLIN'S CAPTURE

Although many stories end well, another one that didn't is the story of Seth Concklin's attempt to rescue Peter Still's family from slavery in Alabama. Peter Still, the brother of William Still of the Philadelphia Underground Railroad, had escaped from an Alabama plantation earlier. Peter returned to Alabama in an unsuccessful attempt to rescue his wife and children. Concklin, who was also a member of the Philadelphia Underground Railroad, volunteered to go to Alabama to help Peter's family escape. Concklin pretended that he was a slave-owner traveling with his servants.

On his first visit to Alabama, Concklin had decided that the steamboats on the Tennessee River were not sufficiently reliable to be depended upon in the escape. He returned to Indiana and made arrangments for assistance in transporting Peter's family across the state to safety in Canada.

Concklin returned to Alabama and then spent seven days and nights in a rowboat escorting Peter Still's family northward across the Ohio River into Indiana. They passed safely through Princeton, Indiana, but were captured twenty-three miles north of Vincennes by a party of men who took them to jail. The marshal at Evansville received a telegram to look out for them. He and their master went to Vincennes and claimed the fugitives, and Concklin was taken away in chains.

Later, Concklin "was found drowned, with his hands and feet in chains and his skull fractured." Reports of the incident claimed that Concklin drowned at the mouth of the Cumberland River at its confluence with the Ohio River, but didn't explain how Concklin's skull had been fractured. He was one of the martyrs of the Underground Railroad movement.

\* \* \*

## WILLIAM "BOX" JONES' STORY

In April 1859, William Jones was a twenty-five-year-old, under-average-size slave owned by a Baltimore commission merchant and grocer. He was not a cruel master, but he was selling off his slaves one at a time; Jones was uncertain about his future. Jones had been treated well, but he disliked the word "slave-holder" and knew that there was no security when one man was owned by another.

William asked a relative to place him in a box, secure the lid, and forward him to Philadelphia via the Erricson Steamship Line. Unfortunately, the size of the box required him to be bent double. He experienced cramps while enroute and was in extreme pain.

On several occasions, he was tempted to cry out in misery. Initially, he controlled himself, but then he grew faint and became exhausted. He thought that he was going to die, but his faith sustained him. Eventually, he revived somewhat and then began to have cold chills. Again, he was in agony. He actually fell asleep, and the chills didn't subside until he awoke.

Jones arrived in Philadelphia on Sunday, where a friend met him at the dock with a hired carriage. The friend knew that freight wasn't delivered on Sunday, but he hoped to convince the cargo officer to allow him to pick up his cargo. He handed the bill of lading to the officer who said, "No, we do not deliver freight on Sunday." However, noticing that the man seemed worried, the officer asked him if he would be able to identify his cargo if he saw it. The friend said that he would, and they went to look for it. They found it quickly; the officer checked it against the bill of lading and authorized the friend to take it with him.

However, the box was too large to be hauled by the hired carriage, and the driver refused to deliver it. The friend spent another hour and a half looking for a larger wagon. Finally, he hired a furniture wagon, and, when he lifted the box, heard a cough from inside it. Fortunately, the driver of the wagon didn't hear the cough and had no concern about the box's contents. The driver dropped off his cargo and went on his way.

The friend and two helpers from the Vigilance Committee, pried the lid off the box. Jones was helped out of, and the rejoicing began. Jones was relieved to be able to stand up straight, and he was overjoyed to be free after seventeen hours in the box. The celebrating continued for several hours. Jones had been ready to scream out in agony just before the lid was removed from his temporary prison. The Underground Railroad helped him travel to Canada and freedom by way of Albany.

*   *   *

## WILLIAM AND ELLEN CRAFT, SERVANT AND MASTER

Georgia slaves William and Ellen Craft, who were husband and wife, knew that they wanted to escape from their bondage, but they weren't sure how to do it. Finally, they decided to attempt escape to the North by traveling as master and servant. Ellen, who was fair enough to pass for white, would pretend to be a young planter traveling with her servant, William. She would dress in fashionable male attire with her hair cut in the style worn by young plantation masters.

Ellen would travel with a muffler around her face, simulating a toothache, to hide her beardless face. Another problem was Ellen's inability to write, for she would need to register at the hotels at which they stayed. Placing Ellen's right arm in a sling took care of that problem. They would portray Ellen as a young master with numerous afflictions, including being hard of hearing and requiring a cane for support. Dark glasses rounded out her disguise. The young master would be very dependent on the faithful servant.

William was suited to carrying out his part of the ruse. He was smart, could think for himself, and was very alert to the needs of his indisposed master. He became the eyes, ears, hands, and feet for his traveling companion. All the young master had to do was to appear to be superior. If anyone attempted to strike up a conversation with him, he would remain mute while his servant explained that his master had

48

a hearing problem.

William and Ellen stayed at a first-class hotel in Charleston and at another expensive hotel in Richmond without any problems. In Baltimore, they went to the railroad station to buy tickets to Philadelphia where William attempted to buy a ticket for his master and himself. Obtaining a ticket for his master wasn't a problem, but he was told that "bonds will have to be entered before you can get a ticket." The ticket master said, "It is a rule of this office to require bonds for all Negroes applying for tickets to the North, and none but gentlemen of well-known responsibility will be taken."

William said that he knew nothing about this requirement, but that he was merely traveling with his master to take care of him. His master was traveling to Philadelphia to seek medical treatment, and it wasn't clear whether he was in sound enough health to complete his journey. William concluded by saying, "My master can't be detained." The station master agreed to waive the rules under the circumstances. William and Ellen were relieved to board the train for Philadelphia.

Upon their arrival in Philadelphia, the muffler was shed, the sling was unslung from the right arm, the dark glasses were removed, and the cane was cast aside. The friends with whom they stayed were happy to observe the blind see, the deaf hear, the toothache cured, and the lame walk without difficulty. Ellen's cure was immediate. She exchanged her black suit, cape, and boots for feminine attire in which she looked attractive and at ease. However, the strain and tension of the trip affected her. She spent several days in bed on her arrival in the North to recover from the pressure under which she had strained.

William and Ellen moved to Boston, where there was less likelihood of being found by slave-catchers and returned to the South. When the Fugitive Slave Law was passed in 1850, it was unlawful to prevent the recapture of slaves. Many slaves fled to Canada at this time. William and Mary decided to stay in Boston and to defend themselves from capture if required. Abolitionist Theodore Parker gave William a pistol and a knife, and suggested that he use them on anyone who attempted to capture them.

Slave-catchers arrived in Boston to attempt to return William and Ellen to their owners. However, the couple were warned in advance. Friends suggested that they travel to England to avoid capture. They took the advice of their friends and lived comfortably in England for twenty years.

*   *   *

## THE YOUNG WOMAN WHO ESCAPED IN A BOX

During the winter of 1857, a twenty-one-year-old African-American seamstress, who was owned by a wealthy Baltimore family, ran away when sent on an errand to complete the arrangements for the Grand Opening Ball at the Academy of Music. A large reward was offered for her return. A free black woman who did the family's washing was thought to have knowledge of the young woman's hiding place. When she failed to divulge any information, she was discharged. In fact, the young seamstress had escaped by being packed into a box and shipped north by a young friend.

Her friend transported the box to the freight depot in Baltimore and paid to have it shipped to Philadelphia. The young woman used a pair of scissors that she had brought with her to make holes in the box to obtain air. The box remained at the depot all night and arrived at Philadelphia about 10:00 a.m. the following morning, after having been turned upside down on more than one occasion.

Her friend arrived at the depot in Philadelphia ahead of the shipment and arranged for a driver to deliver it to Mrs. Myer's house near Minster Street. The driver, observing that the young man was anxious to have the box delivered promptly, persuaded the freight agent to release the shipment to them early.

The friend had told the addressee, Mrs. Myers, about the contents of the box. She was overwhelmed with the responsibility that had been thrust upon her and was concerned about the well-being of the box's contents. She invited the undertaker's shrouder, Mrs. Ash, to be present when the box was opened, in case the young woman had not survived the shipment. The two women pried off the lid and looked at the young woman in the straw, but could see no sign of life. They thought that their worst fears were realized, and that they were looking at a corpse.

They spoke to the young woman and asked to her to stand up. She began to show faint signs of life. She could not speak and had to be helped out of the box. Finally, she said, "I feel so deadly weak." They asked if she would like something to eat or drink, but she declined at first. Eventually, she agreed to having a cup of tea.

She went to bed and stayed there all day. She gained strength during the second day, but still didn't have much to say. On the third day, the young woman began to be herself and to talk freely. She had difficulty describing her discomfort and her fears in the box. Her principal fear was being discovered and being sent back to slavery.

The young woman spent three or four days at Mrs. Myers' house and then a similar period at the home of William Still, a leader in the Underground Railroad in Philadelphia. She was helped on her way to Canada and freedom. Of all the slaves who had attempted to escape by being shipped in a box, this young woman came as close as any of them to dying enroute. Her situation had been complicated by the fact that she was pregnant. If her friend in Baltimore had realized her condition, he probably would not have let her attempt that means of escape.

\* \* \*

Greystone Inn, Lansing

# CHAPTER 3

# Underground Railroad Tales
## of the
## New England States

"I am aware that many object to the severity of my language; but is there not cause for severity? I will be as harsh as truth, and as compromising as justice. On this subject, I do not wish to think, or speak, or write with moderation. No! No! Tell a man whose house is on fire to give a moderate alarm; tell him to moderately rescue his wife from the hands of a ravisher; tell the mother to gradually extricate her babe from the fire into which it has fallen—but urge me not to use moderation in a cause [antislavery] like the present, I am in earnest—I will not equivocate—I will not excuse—I will not retreat a single inch—AND I WILL BE HEARD."

William Lloyd Garrison,
*Editor of the abolitionist newspaper,* Liberator

53

## AUSTIN BEARSE'S STORY

Austin Bearse, a native of Massachusetts, was a mate on various sailing ships from New England that plied the coast of South Carolina during the winters from 1818 to 1830. The ships carried cotton and rice from plantations along the rivers to markets in Charleston. The ships also delivered slaves gathered by the slave-traders in Charleston to the river plantations. The slaves were sold for many reasons: the death of an owner, the division of an estate, a reduction in the number of domestics required, and as punishment for refusing to obey orders. Additionally, when plantation owners moved to the West or the North, they usually sold their slaves rather than taking them with them.

The ships carried anywhere from two or three to seventy or eighty slaves. Many were separated from their familes, and their owners didn't seem to care. Ships carrying slaves would usually tie up at Poor Man's Hole outside of Charleston, and relatives and friends were allowed to come on board for the night. When the ship left in the morning, much heart-wrenching weeping and wailing was heard as relatives left the ship, and families were broken up.

In 1847, Bearse sailed to Albany where he visited the Mott sisters, who were active in the antislavery movement. They had hidden a slave, George Lewis, who was in danger of recapture. They wanted him transported to Boston because a writ had been processed for his capture in Albany. George was hidden on board the ship until they passed New York City; he was allowed to come on deck when they entered Long Island Sound. He arrived safely in Boston, where he began a new life.

One evening in 1854, Wendell Phillips, the Boston abolitionist, and two of his friends came to Bearse's house to tell him about a schooner from Wilmington, North Carolina, that had tied up at Fort Independence with an escaped slave on board. The schooner was the *Sally Ann* out of Belfast, Maine, with a load of yellow pine for Boston customers. Phillips and his friends had told Bearse that the captain of the schooner wanted to unload his refugee passenger.

That night Bearse sailed his yacht alongside the *Sally Ann*, hailed her, and asked the captain if he was ready to give up the slave that he had on board. The schooner's captain answered, "If you come alongside my vessel, I will send you to eternity—quick!" Bearse sailed to Long Wharf and waited for three hours. Then he fastened a dozen old hats and jackets to the railing along one side of his vessel to give the appearance of having a large crew. Bearse again maneuvered alongside the *Sally Ann*, told her captain that he had come with help this time, and said that he could prevent bloodshed if he gave up the fugitive.

After some initial resistance, the schooner's captain lowered the slave into a small boat that Bearse's brother rowed under the bow of the *Sally Ann*. They climbed aboard Bearse's yacht, which made for City Point in South Boston.

Bearse brought the slave to his house and gave him a change of clothing. At daybreak, two conductors of the Underground Railroad pulled up at Bearse's house in a carriage to take the slave to the Boston and Worcester Railroad depot. One of the conductors went with the runaway to Worcester, where he was transported to safety in Canada by the Underground Railroad.

In October, 1854, Wendell Phillips and another member of the antislavery movement came to Bearse's house at City Point, South Boston, with news of a slave on board the brig, *Cameo*, of Augusta, Maine. The brig was delivering a load of pine lumber from Jacksonville, Florida, and was tied up somewhere in Boston. Bearse, his brother, and other members of the Vigilance Committee searched the waterfront for the brig. Bearse searched City Point and Neponset, and his brother checked Boston Wharf as far as Long Wharf.

When they met the next morning at the headquarters of the Vigilance Committee, Bearse's brother told him that he had found the brig and the slave at Boston Wharf. The Vigilance Committee obtained a search warrant to search the *Cameo;* they went to Boston Wharf, where they boarded the vessel with the constable. The mate gave them permission to search, but they didn't find the slave. Bearse went down the aft hatch and found the bed on top of the lumber where the slave had rested on the journey to Boston. Another member of the Vigilance Committe called Bearse up on deck and said, "Look at that vessel on the opposite side of the dock. I think the slave we want is there."

Bearse boarded the schooner, *William*, and, as he went on board, all of the crew left. The slave was on board the *William*, whose owners also owned the *Cameo*. He had been given a change of clothing from his slave dress of tow cloth, and the schooner had been preparing to leave the wharf. The runaway was being taken back to his master in the South. Bearse asked him if he was a slave, and he didn't reply. When Bearse asked him if he came to Boston in the *Cameo*, he said that he did. He said that the captain had threatened to throw him overboard off Cape Cod if he showed himself on deck.

Bearse told the fugitive that he was now among friends, and that he was a free man. He was happy to leave the schooner with the Vigilance Committee members, who drove him in a carriage to Lewis Haydn's home on Southac Street. The constable turned in his search warrant with the comment, "No slave found on board the *Cameo*." The refugee stayed at Hadyn's house for two weeks, until they noticed that the house was being watched by a constable and a policeman.

They dressed the escaped slave in women's clothing, and William Bowditch of Brookline moved him by carriage to Mr. Allen's house in Concord via East Cambridge, Somerville, and Medford. The slave was transported by the Underground Railroad to Canada, where he lived for nine years before returning to Boston after the signing of the Emancipation Proclamation.

*   *   *

## HENRY "BOX" BROWN'S STORY

Henry Brown, a slave from Richmond, Virginia, knew that he was going to travel to the North to escape slavery, but he didn't know how he was going to do it. He considered traveling on foot during the night, and he thought about going to the coast and trying to obtain passage on a boat. Brown knew of the risks associated with those two means of travel. Runaway slaves were frequently captured and returned to their masters for punishment. He decided to try a different mode of travel.

Brown asked Samuel A. Smith, a white Richmond carpenter, to make box for him, place him in it, and ship him to Philadelphia. Brown ordered a box three feet long, two feet wide, and two feet, eight inches deep lined with napped cotton with the appearance of felt. His only sustenance was two biscuits and a small container filled with water. He carried a large gimlet to bore breathing holes in the box.

Brown climbed into the box, which was nailed shut and bound with five hickory hoops. His friend, James A. Smith, a shoe merchant, addressed the box to William H. Johnson, Arch Street, Philadelphia, and marked on it "This side up with care." The box was transported to the Adams' Express Office in a wagon and then by overland express for twenty-six hours to Philadelphia. The notice, "This side up with care," was ignored by the expressmen who handled the box roughly and placed it upside down, with Brown on his head, for many miles.

The day before the box arrrived in Philadelphia, a member of the Vigilance Committee who helped runaway slaves, checked the Adams' Express Depot for a box that might hold a slave; he didn't find any. The next afternoon, J. Miller McKim, a leader in the Underground Railroad movement, received a telegram from Richmond with the message "Your goods is shipped and will arrive tomorrow morning." McKim decided to have the box delivered directly to the Anti-Slavery Office, instead of putting a member of the Vigilance Committee at risk by picking it up at the depot.

However, having the box delivered to the Anti-Slavery Office might also raise suspicion. McKim consulted his businessman friend, E. M. Davis, who suggested that he have the box delivered by Dan the Irishman, a reliable driver at the Adams' Express Office who made frequent deliveries for his company. Dan was asked to deliver the box the following morning and was given a five-dollar gold piece for his troubles.

Gathered at the Anti-Slavery office the following morning were McKim, Professor C. D. Cleveland, William Still, who was a leader of Philadelphia's Underground Railroad, and Lewis Thompson of Merrihew & Thompson, the printers of many antislavery pamphlets. The box was delivered, the door was locked, and the four men stood around the box as though they were about to witness the Resurrection. McKim knocked on the top of the box and asked, "All right?" The answer came from the box, "All right, sir."

They used a hatchet and saw to undo the hickory loops and then pried the lid off the box. Brown stood up, extended his hand, and said, "How do you do gentlemen?" The four men were at a loss for words as they looked at Brown, who was dripping with perspiration. Brown told them that before leaving Richmond he had chosen a psalm to sing if he arrived safely in Philadelphia. It began with the words: "I waited patiently for the Lord, and He heard my prayer." The men were touched as Brown sang the psalm to them.

Brown, known from this time on as Henry "Box" Brown, moved to Boston, where he became an active member of the Underground Railroad helping other slaves escape. Samuel A. Smith, the white carpenter who made the box for Brown and placed him in it, was not so fortunate. He didn't get caught helping Brown, but he was caught aiding two other "boxed" slaves in escaping. Smith was convicted and imprisoned for eight years for his part in their attempted escape.

\* \* \*

## INCIDENTS IN THE LIFE OF A SLAVE GIRL

Harriet Jacobs was born near Edenton, North Carolina, in 1815. Her parents died while she was a child. Upon the death of her mistress, who had taught her to read, she was sent to an immoral master who subjected her to unending sexual abuse as she grew into adolescence. Jacobs bore two children to another white man while still in her teens. Her master became jealous and attempted to make her a concubine. She ran away and hid in the home of her grandmother, who was a freed slave. The father of her children bought them from their owner and brought them to live with their mother. However, he didn't follow through on his promise to buy their freedom.

In 1842, Jacobs escaped with her daughter and son to New York, where she found work as a nursemaid for the family of a wealthy publisher. She moved to Boston when she heard that she was being pursued as a fugitive in New York. Jacobs accompanied the publisher's family on a trip to England to visit their relatives. Upon her return, she planned to settle in Boston where she felt safer from the pursuit of slave-holders than she did in New York. However, her son had left his apprenticeship in Boston and had shipped out on a sailing vessel.

Instead of staying in Boston as she had planned, she moved to Rochester, New York, to live with her brother in 1849. Her brother, John S. Jacobs, was a fugitive who was active in the abolitionist movement. Rochester was a fast-growing town on the Erie Canal and the home of Frederick Douglass' *North Star*, an abolitionist newspaper. Jacobs ran an antislavery reading room, where she met many of the reformers of the day, including Amy Post who helped her with her writing.

In September, 1850, Jacobs returned to New York to work for the family of the publisher for whom she had previously worked. She was again pursued by slave-holders until her employer purchased her and her two children and freed them.

In 1861, Jacobs' narrative of her experiences as a slave, *Incidents in the Life of a Slave Girl: Written by Herself,* was published in Boston. Jacobs' book addressed a subject in her book that had not previously been placed before the public—the sexual harassment of female slaves. She described her feelings on writing about the subject in a letter to Amy Post:

> I have, dear friend, striven faithfully to give a true and just account of my own life in slavery. God knows I have tried to do it in a Christian spirit. There are some things that I might have made plainer, I know. Woman can whisper her cruel wrongs into the ear of a very dear friend easier than she can record them for the world to read. I have left nothing out but what I thought the world might believe that a slave woman was too willing to pour out, that she might gain their sympathies. I ask nothing. I have placed myself before you to be judged as a woman, whether I deserve your pity or contempt.

Jacobs was sufficiently concerned about the subject matter that she used the pseudonym, Linda Brent. William C. Nell, an African-American reviewer for the abolitionist newspaper, *The Liberator,* wrote:

> ... the oft-told tale of American slavery, in another and more revolting phase than is generally seen: More revolting because it is of the spirit and not the flesh. In this volume, a woman tells ... not how she was scourged and maimed, but that far more terrible sufferings endured by and inflicted upon women, by a system that legalizes concubinage, and offers a premium to licentiousness.

The narrative includes the story of Jacobs' struggle to prevent her master from raping her, her plans for escape, and her journey to freedom. She also discusses her love for another slave whom she was not permitted to marry. She appeals to female readers "whose purity has been sheltered from childhood, who have been free to choose the objects of your affection, whose homes are protected by law, do not judge the poor desolate slave girl too severely."

Jacobs describes how, in attempting to prevent her master forcing her into concubinage, she surrenders her "purity" in order to retain her "self-respect." She stopped attempting to avoid sexual involvement in order to prevent being "entirely subject to the will of another." She described her feelings at the time: "It seems less degrading to give one's self, than to submit to compulsion. There is something akin to freedom in having a lover who has no control over you, except that which he gains by kindness and attachment. Still, in looking back, calmly, on the events of my life, I feel that the slave woman ought not be judged by the same standard as others."

During the Civil War, Jacobs worked as a nurse for African-American troops in Washington, D.C. She was active in work among the freed slaves for thirty years after the war. She died in Washington, D.C., in 1897.

\* \* \*

## James Mars' Story

Reverend Thompson of North Canaan, Connecticut, married a woman from Loudon County, Virginia, and moved her and her slaves, including James Mars' mother, to Canaan. James' mother fell in love with a slave named Mars from New York State, and Reverend Thompson performed their wedding ceremony. James was their oldest child. His half-brother, Joseph, was from his mother's first marriage.

Life went smoothly for a brief time, until Mrs. Thompson began to mistreat the Mars family. She told James' father that if they were living in Virginia, where she would have at her call a dozen men, she would have him stripped and flogged until his skin was hanging in strings.

Mrs. Thompson said that then Mars would do what she asked.

She told him, "You mind, boy, I will have you there yet, and you will get your pay for all that you have done." However, James' father was a strongly built man and did not frighten easily. James' mother told James that she had often seen her mother tied up and flogged until her blood flowed across the floor.

As relations between the North and the South became more strained, Reverend and Mrs. Thompson planned to move to Virginia, leaving the operation of the Connecticut farm to the Mars family. James' father could not accept the possibility of being separated from his wife, daughter, and two sons. One night he loaded up the Thompson's wagon and moved his family to Norfolk, which was known as an antislavery town.

The first night they stayed at Pettibone's tavern, whose owner aided fugitive slaves. The tavern owner referred them to a man named Phelps who owned an unoccupied house in a remote area. After they had lived there for several months, they heard that the Thompsons were planning to recapture their slaves, particularly James and his brother Joseph.

Their next door neighbor, Mrs. Cady, offered to take the boys into town to the Tibbals house, where they would be safer. An old man, a middle-aged man and his wife, and four children lived at the Tibbals house. Since Joseph was fourteen, six years older than James, the searchers would be looking harder for him to put him to work. Mr. Butler, who was visiting the neighborhood, offered to take Joseph to Massachusetts with him. James returned to the Phelps house, where his parents were staying.

While Joseph and James were gone, Reverend Thompson had visited their mother at the Phelps house with a proposal: "If she would go to Canaan and see to his things and pack them up for him, then if she didn't want to go [to Virginia], she need not." However, Reverend Thompson still wasn't happy; he wanted Joseph back. The Mars family again packed their possessions into Thompson's wagon and returned to Norfolk, where they stayed overnight in Captain Lawrence's tavern. Lawrence recommended that the family disperse and then keep moving to avoid detection.

Initially, James stayed with a woman in the neighborhood of the tavern. He said, "I stopped with her a few days with instructions to keep still. You may wonder why I was sent to such a place; most likely it was thought that she had so little room that she would not be suspected of harboring a fugitive." A man named Walter, who stopped by to check up on him from time to time, told him that if anyone came to the door "he must get under the bed." From there, he moved around to the Pease house, the Atkins house, the Foot house, and then to the home of another Atkins family.

Eventually, the boys were returned to Reverend Thompson. He decided to sell both Joseph and James, but he allowed their parents to select the owner to whom they would be sold. Mr. Munger of Norfolk paid $100 for James, and Mr. Bingham of Salisbury paid the same amount for Joseph. Their parents and sister were set free, and Joseph was a slave until he turned twenty-five. James, upon the death of Mr. Munger, was set free at the age of twenty-one. James married, settled in Norfolk, and had a long, productive life.

* * *

## "Mister" Clarissa Davis

In May 1854, Clarissa Davis escaped with two of her brothers from her owners in Portsmouth, Virginia. Her brothers' escape was successful, but her attempt failed. Clarissa was twenty-two years old, attractive, modest, and well-spoken despite having limited schooling. A $1,000 reward had been offered for her capture and that of her brothers.

Clarissa's brothers settled in New Bedford, Massachussetts, and waited for her. Clarissa's owners were Mrs. Brown and Mrs. Burkley; she had known no other owners. Clarissa acknowledged that she "had not been used as hard as many others were."

She made several other unsuccessful attempts to escape. Finally, two and a half months after her brothers had fled, she received word that the *City of Richmond* had arrived from Philadelphia. William Bagnel, a steward on board the ship who was a friend, offered to help her escape.

Clarissa was told that the ship would leave Portsmouth at dawn, and that she should board about 3:00 a.m. She prayed for rain that would keep some of the policemen off the streets. Just before three o'clock she dressed in male attire, and her prayers were answered— the rain that had begun at midnight continued. She reached the ship safely, and   Bagnel hid her in a large box on board the *City of*

*Richmond.*

Clarissa arrived in Philadelphia without incident, and the vigilance committee helped her on her way to join her brothers in New Bedford. They recommended that she change her name to help avoid recapture. She chose the name Mary D. Armistead. Later, the Underground Railroad also helped her father, who was old and infirm, escape. Clarissa, or "Mary," was very appreciative of the support that she had received from the Underground Railroad. She maintained her contacts with those who had helped her on her way to freedom.

\* \* \*

## Moses Roper's Story

Moses Roper was born into slavery in Caswell County, North Carolina. In his early teens, he worked mixing medicines for Dr. Jones, who was a cotton planter and a medical doctor, and briefly worked as a journeyman tailor. He was sold to another master and assigned to work in the fields. He had difficulty keeping up with the other slaves because he wasn't used to the hard labor. He was whipped frequently for being too slow. He repeatedly attempted to escape, was caught, and received 100 lashes for each escape attempt.

After many attempts to run away, Roper was flogged 500 times and chained in a log pen with a forty-pound chain that was used to drag logs from the woods. After his next attempt to escape, he was chained for a week to an eighteen-year-old female slave, who had been captured while running away. The chain wasn't removed until the weekend. They were frequently flogged because they could not keep up with the work pace of the other slaves. He was embarrassed to be chained to the young woman, but he was more concerned that she should be treated in such a fashion.

Upon being recaptured after another escape attempt, Roper was stripped naked, hung up on a rail in a log house, and given 200 lashes. Then he was taken to the blacksmith shop where a twenty-pound ring was put on his ankles, and he was chained again to the same woman to whom he had been chained before. The chained pair escaped from the cotton fields, and Roper managed to pound off the chain with a large stone. They found a canoe, crossed a river, and asked for food at a nearby house. The people at the house helped Roper remove the rings around his ankles. He decided that he and the young slave woman should travel in different directions. He was concerned that if they were captured together, she would be forced to tell who had helped to remove the rings from his ankles.

Roper had witnessed a cruel form of punishment while working on a plantation in South Carolina. The master drove nails into a barrel so that the point of the nails extended into the interior of the barrel. He placed one of his slaves into the barrel and rolled the barrel down a hill. One master killed six or seven of his slaves in this way.

Roper observed another inhuman form of punishment administered to one of the female slaves on the plantation. She was given as much castor oil and salts as she could drink. Then she was covered with a box six feet long, two and a half feet wide, and one and a half feet deep. The master had his men place many heavy logs on top of the box and left the slave inside until the next morning. Roper said that this woman had received 3,000 lashes over a period of time.

Finally, Roper decided to escape by steamboat and traveled to Savannah. He had no pass to show that he was a freed slave. He told a young man that he had lost it and asked the young man to write him out another one. The pass didn't look very official, so he made a point of letting it get wet when he crossed the next river. He showed the blurred pass to a cotton planter who wrote out a new one for him that looked much more official than the previous one.

A steward on one of the New York packets in Savannah knew Captain DeKay of the schooner *Fox,* and obtained a position for Roper on that schooner. The *Fox* was an old vessel loaded with cattle and lumber for the New York market. After a four-day delay, Roper left the *Fox* and boarded a brig bound for Providence. However, the captain of the brig refused to take Roper on as an assistant steward because he suspected that he was a runaway slave. Roper returned to the *Fox;* the captain hadn't found a replacement and was willing to take Roper back. In six days, the *Fox* arrived at Staten Island, where they were quarantined for two days.

Roper was unable to find work either in New York or in the surrounding countryside. He went back on board the *Fox,* which was bound for Poughkeepsie. He found a temporary job at an inn there. Roper thought that he might have better luck at finding a job in Albany, so he boarded a steamboat to travel farther up the Hudson

River. Finding no employment in Albany, he obtained passage on a canalboat bound for Vermont.

Roper found the people in Vermont hospitable and kind, and he was able to find a job in Sudbury. From Sudbury, he moved to Ludlow, where he stayed with the deacon of a church. He lived briefly in New Hampshire before moving to Boston, where he worked in a shop. In Boston, two African-American men told Roper that inquiries were being made about him, and that a reward was being offered for information leading to his capture.

Roper liked New England and wanted to stay there, but he feared for his safety. He hid in the Green Mountains for several weeks and then returned to New York, where he boarded the *Napoleon* bound for Liverpool. Roper was given refuge in England, and he remained there. He bore no ill will to the land of his birth:

> Whatever I may have experienced in America, at the hands of cruel taskmasters, yet I am unwilling to speak in any but respectful terms of the land of my birth. It is far from my wish to attempt to degrade America in the eyes of Britons. I love her institutions in the free states, her zeal for Christ; I bear no enmity even to the slave-holders, but regret their delusions, many I am aware are deeply sensible of the fault, but some I regret to say are not, and I could wish to open their eyes to their sin....

\* \* \*

## NEHEMIAH CAULKINS' STORY

Nehemiah Caulkins lived on a plantation near Wilmington, North Carolina, from 1824 until 1835. As a slave, he observed many cases of mistreatment of other slaves by their masters. On one occasion, an overseer approached a slave in the field who had been accused of stealing a suckling pig. The slave, suspecting that he was about to be punished for stealing the pig, dropped his hoe and ran for the nearby woods. He hadn't run far when the overseer aimed his loaded shotgun at him, fired, and brought him down.

The wounded slave was carried by his friends to the plantation infirmary and the neighborhood doctor was called. The doctor removed much of the duck shot from his wound. The slave couldn't return to work for six weeks until his wounds were healed. Caulkins examined the wounded slave's body when he returned to work in the fields; twenty-six pellets had been left in him.

On another occasion, Caulkins observed a runaway slave, Harry, who had been captured and placed in the stocks. The stocks were built with two heavy pieces of lumber over ten feet long and seven inches wide. The pieces had semi-circular cuts in which to place the ankles and were hinged at one end and secured with a clasp and a lock at the other. The slave sat on the floor of the barn and was locked in position, where he was left day and night for a week. He was flogged every morning.

During the second week Harry was removed from the stocks each morning, and a heavy logging chain was fastened around his neck with the ends of the chain dragging on the ground. He worked during the day in the fields with the other slaves and was locked in the stocks again each night.

Caulkins also saw women slaves being whipped. Old Ben, a religious man, was given the odious task of whipping his fellow slaves. One of the mistress' daughters sent a seventeen-year-old woman slave to Ben one day to be whipped. The young slave had displeased her young mistress, who then boxed her ears and beat her. As she hit her, the mistress scratched her finger on a pin in the young slave girl's dress. She sent her to Ben for worse punishment.

Ben could always be heard praying before each flogging. As he beat his fellows, he cried out: "Poor African slave! Poor African slave!" After the flogging, Caulkins asked Ben whether he made the young girl strip before her flogging. Ben replied that he made both men and women strip before receiving their lashes. He explained that he didn't used to ask women to strip. Once a female slave returned to the house after her flogging, and the mistress examined her back for welts and didn't find any. Ben was ordered to have female slaves strip before being whipped, otherwise he would be flogged himself.

After observing this abuse of his fellow human beings, Caulkins needed no futher motivation to run away from the plantation. He escaped to the North with the help of the Underground Railroad. Caulkins settled and lived happily in Waterford, Connecticut.

# Tales of the
# Finger Lakes Region

"*The flight was a bold and perilous one, but here I am, in the great city of New York, safe and sound, with out the loss of blood or bone. A free state around me, a free earth under my feet! What a moment this was to me! A whole year was pressed into single day. A world upon my agitated vision. It was a moment of joyous excitement which no words can describe. Sensations are too intense and too rapid for words. Joy and gladness, like the rainbow of promise, defy alike the pen and pencil ...*"

*Frederick Douglass*

## The Escape of Jermain Loguen

Jermain Loguen was born a slave on a small plantation on Manskers Creek, sixteen miles northeast of Nashville, Tennessee. His owner was Elinor Telford, a widow who ran the farm with her sons, Manasseh, Carnes, and David. The Telfords acquired another slave, Cherry, when she was seven years old. In her teens, Cherry became the mistress of David, the youngest Telford son. They had four children, Maria, Jermain, Ann, and Jane.

In 1816, David married Polly Glascoe and lost interest in Cherry. Manasseh and Carnes frequently beat her, particularly after their visits to the plantation's distillery, which was one of their businesses. During his formative years, Jermain saw his mother "knocked down with clubs, stripped and bound, and flogged with sticks, ox whips and rawhides until the blood streamed down the gashes upon her body."

One day Manasseh sold two of Cherry's children. She ran after the men taking her children away, but was dragged back to the house and chained to a heavy loom. Physically she recovered, but the wounds to her spirit remained. She became increasingly nervous.

Shortly after this incident, Jermain saw Sam, his friend and the slave of a neighbor, stripped, tied to a barrel, and beaten with a "board shaped like a huge Yankee pudding stick filled with small auger holes, and of a heft to do the most execution upon the flesh it bruises." Then Sam was kicked after he became unconscious, and the barrel was rolled down a steep embankment. His body was carried home from the bottom of the hill. Jermain was saddened by the brutal death of Sam, who had saved him from drowning previously.

Jermain began to save money for his escape. He bought a barrel of whiskey at wholesale and used Manasseh's ox team to transport the barrel to town to retail it. Manasseh returned early from a visit to their preacher's house and saw Jermain returning the ox team to the barn. He tried to tie up Jermain and whip him, but Jermain wouldn't allow it. He threw Manesseh "half a rod onto his head" and ran into the nearby woods. He lived in the woods for three weeks on food supplied by his friend, John Farney.

Finally, Jermain realized that the only way to prepare for his escape was to return to the plantation. He returned and told Manasseh that he was ready to go back to work. Manasseh, without comment, put him to work making fences. Shortly after he returned, his sister, Maria, was sold. Her husband and three children never saw her again. Jermain could no longer endure the conditions of slavery.

Jermain and Farney had saved some money and had forged passes for freed slaves. On Christmas Eve, 1834, the two men, armed with guns that they had purchased, set out on their master's finest horses, which they had groomed carefully for their journey. They were lucky when crossing the Cumberland River into Kentucky. The tollgate keeper had left a young boy in charge who didn't question them as he should have, since word of their escape had been published in regional newspapers. They crossed the Ohio River on the ice and had to evade a mob on the Indiana shore.

The two runaways talked to an African-American who told them that they wouldn't be safe until they arrived in Canada. He directed them to a friend in Corydon, Indiana, who sent them to Beck's Mill Settlement in Washington County. From there, they were helped by James Overrals in Indianapolis who forwarded them to a Quaker settlement north of the city enroute to Logansport, Indiana. They crossed into Michigan, where they became lost but were saved from the severe winter by Native Americans.

Jermain and Farney went separate ways prior to crossing the Detroit River. Jermain arrived in Windsor, Ontario, with fifty cents in his pocket and a tired mare. He couldn't find work in Windsor, Chatham, or London, Ontario, but was hired to cut wood and split rails in Hamilton. Eventually, he made his way to New York State where he attended the Oneida Institute and became a minister in the African Methodist Episcopal Church, a vocal abolitionist, and a leader in the Underground Railroad in Syracuse.

\* \* \*

## ESCAPE IN A SEA CHEST

*"$150 REWARD—Ran away from the subscriber, on Sunday night, 27th inst., my NEGRO GIRL, Lear Green, about 18 years of age, black complexion, round featured, good-looking and ordinary size.... The above reward will be paid if said girl is taken out of the State of Maryland and delivered to me; or fifty dollars if taken in the State of Maryland."*

*JAMES NOBLE, No. 153 Broadway, Baltimore*

69

James Noble, the butter dealer who placed this advertisement in the Baltimore *Sun*, inherited Lear Green from his wife's mother, Mrs. Rachel Howard. Lear's new mistress, Mrs. Noble, who was demanding and oppressive, allowed her few liberties. While Lear worked for Mrs. Noble, a slave, William Adams, proposed to her. Lear wanted to accept his proposal, but she didn't want to have the burden of marriage and children added to the burden of slavery. Lear's mother advised her to escape from slavery before she undertook the responsibilities of marriage.

Lear and her mother decided to ship Lear north in a chest. They found an old sea chest, which they packed with a pillow, a few articles of clothing, some food, and a water bottle. Lear climbed in, the lid was closed, and strong ropes were tied around the chest. The chest was shipped north on an Erricson Lines steamship. Lear's future mother-in-law, a free woman, offered to accompany the chest on its journey. The Erricson Line assigned black passengers to the deck, which was where the chest was stored. The deck was precisely where Mrs. Adams wanted to be to keep an eye on the chest.

On several occasions during the middle of the night, Mrs. Adams unbound the ropes from the chest and raised the lid to allow Lear to get some fresh air. The young woman and Mrs. Adams prayed together for their enterprise to end safely. Lear claimed that she experienced no fear. The ship reached Philadelphia without incident, and the chest was off-loaded at the wharf and delivered to a friend's house. Lear, who spent eighteen hours in the chest, was relieved to step out of the chest and stretch.

Lear and the chest were later transported to the home of William Still, a leader in the Underground Railroad in Philadelphia. Lear stayed in Still's house for several days under the protection of the Vigilance Committee. From Philadelphia, Lear moved to Elmira, where she was married to William Adams. William and Lear established their home in Elmira; they didn't feel the need to travel to Canada to escape the slave-catchers.

\* \* \*

## FREDERICK DOUGLASS, STATIONMASTER

Frederick Douglass was not only a famous abolitionist speaker and editor but also a Rochester stationmaster for the Underground Railroad. He helped hundreds of slaves escape, and none of the fugitives under his care were ever captured. However, they had many close calls.

On one occasion, Douglass was told by the law partner of the United States Commissioner that papers were being prepared for the arrest of three escaped slaves from Maryland. One of the fugitives was hiding at Asa Anthony's farm west of Rochester, a second was housed at the old Quaker settlement in Farmington, and the third was at Douglass' home. Douglass and his friends moved quickly, and, before the arrests could be made, the three men boarded a ship at the Port of Rochester and were on their way across Lake Ontario to safety in Canada.

On another occasion, three fugitives stayed in Rochester for several months. While waiting for passage to Canada, they attended antislavery meetings in Corinthian Hall. Douglass was advised that their master was in town with a warrant for their arrest. The three men were moved around the city for three days while the marshal searched for them. Finally, in the middle of the night, they were given Quaker bonnets and heavy veils, driven to the Port of Rochester in a closed carriage, and placed aboard a ship for passage to Canada.

A third set of three fugitives housed by Douglass were pursued more aggressively than the first two groups because they had killed one slave-catcher and wounded another in Christiana, Pennsylvania, while resisting capture. A large reward was offered for their arrest, and many law officers were searching for them. Douglass' English friend, Julia Griffis, arranged for their passage to Canada on a British ship that was tied up on the Genesee River. The men were disguised in women's clothing, and Douglass personally drove them to the dock in his carriage. They arrived just as the ship was about to leave the pier. Reverend Parker, one of the fugitives, gave Douglass the pistol that had killed the slave-catcher as a souvenir.

Douglass frequently used the African Methodist Episcopal Zion

Church at the corner of Spring and Favor Streets as an Underground Railroad station. Slaves were hidden in the basement and in the pews while arrangements were made to transport them to freedom. Harriet Tubman, the "Moses of her people," was one of the many with whom Douglass worked in helping the escaping slaves.

\* \* \*

## HARRIET'S ESCAPE

In the fall of 1830, John Davenport, a Virginia planter, registered at the Syracuse House with his wife and baby and a young slave girl. The slave girl, Harriet Powell, was an attractive young woman with a complexion as white as her owners, since her father was white. When workers at the hotel found out that Harriet was not a white servant or a relative of the Davenport's but their slave, they talked to local abolitionists about planning her escape.

At first, Harriet disapproved of notion of escaping because the Davenports treated her well. Also, she knew that if the escape attempt failed, she would be "sold South," that is, sold to an owner in a deep south state where working conditions were much tougher. William M. Clarke, the Deputy County Clerk, and John R. Owen, a local marble merchant, conceived of an escape plan, and convinced Harriet that the plan would succeed.

The Davenports planned to return to the South on October 8, and the escape was set for the evening of October 7. Harriet was taking care of the baby during a farewell party for the Davenports in the banquet hall at the hotel. Harriet went downstairs, handed the baby to Mrs. Davenport, and explained that she had to run a brief errand.

Harriet left the hotel by the back door where she was met by Clark and Owen in a carriage. They stopped briefly at an abolitionist meeting at the Congregational Church where money was collected to help Harriet escape. The first stop on the Underground Railroad was at the home of Mr. Sheppard in Marcellus. The next station was the home of Gerrit Smith, a leader in the Underground Railroad movement in Peterboro, Madison County.

When Harriet failed to return from "running her errand," the Davenports notified the authorities, who began a search of the homes of known abolitionists. The Syracuse to Oswego packet boat on the Oswego Canal was searched, and the Davenports circulated handbills offering $200 for her return. However, Harrriet was safely transported from Peterboro to Canada by the efficient Underground Railroad organization.

In the following year, Davenport went bankrupt, and all of his property was sold. If Harriet had not agreed to escape, she would have been sold to new owners who might not have treated her as well as the Davenports did.

\* \* \*

## HIDDEN IN THE WOODPILE

One night in the 1850s, a group of men left the road from Palmyra to Pultneyville and turned onto a secret path along Salmon Creek. As dark clouds scudded across the sky, a conductor on the Underground Railroad led the escaped slaves toward Underground Railroad stations in Pultneyville. They climbed into a large canoe tied up along the shore of Salmon creek and paddled toward the village.

The men crossed Pig Lane and approached the back of three houses. One was directly in front of them and two were off to the left. The house farthest to the left was a cobblestone house, the one next to it was a New England-style frame house, and the one toward which they walked was a small, white salt-box house. All three of these houses overlooked Lake Ontario.

The cobblestone house, 4184 Washington Street, had been built in 1832 by Captain Horatio Throop, who transported escaped slaves across Lake Ontario in his steamships. A two-story brick addition with a cupola was built in later years in front of the small salt-box house at 4194 Washington Street.

As they approached the salt-box house from the rear, the door opened and the conductor led the group toward the stairs at the right side of the back room. The stairs made a right-angle turn on the way to the second floor, and a second right-angle turn led them to a second-floor bedroom. A ladder had been placed under a fifteen-inch by twenty-seven-inch trapdoor in the ceiling of the bedroom.

The conductor directed the slaves to climb the ladder and to hide in the crawl space in the eaves of the attic. The slaves had just enough room to stretch out across the rafters and lie down to sleep. They stayed in the attic during the night when it was cool and in the cellar during the day when the attic was too hot.

A knock on the trapdoor awakened the slaves just before daybreak. They could look out of the small attic windows and see two wharves extending out into Lake Ontario. Several schooners pitched and rolled at their anchors. The steamship *Ontario* was tied up at its dock. The western wharf, which was just east of the mouth of Salmon Creek, had several large warehouses. The warehouses were used to store fruit, fresh meat, potash, and wood to load on ships leaving Pultneyville.

The slaves were led down to the room at the back of the house where they had entered the night before. Diagonally opposite the stairway was a four-foot by six-foot trap door through which they descended into the cellar. While the slaves bided their time in the cellar, the Sessions House across the street was a beehive of activity. Federal employees working there enforced the customs laws of the United States.

As the local Justice of the Peace, the conductor of the night before, entered the Sessions House, he noticed sheriff's men from the South who were there as slave-catchers. At the end of the day, the customs men left the Sessions House and walked to the dock to check Captain Throop's cargo and passenger lists. The sheriff's men hung about the wharf. On the bridge of the *Ontario*, Captain Throop, a talented banjo player, began to play southern melodies. The southerners were drawn to the end of the wharf to listen to the music. They began to call out requests to the captain.

The Justice saw the signal from the *Ontario* and led the slaves across the street, through the cellar of the warehouse, and into the piles of wood that extended from one end of the wharf to the other. The wood, which was fuel for the steamships, had been stacked so that the slaves could move through passageways unobserved by those standing at the other end of the wharf. The Justice walked alongside the woodpiles toward the *Ontario*. He called out to the captain, "Captain Throop, what do you carry?" The captain responded, "My boat runs for passengers." The Justice asked, "Do you have sufficient fuel for the voyage?" This question notified the captain that he had additional passengers in the woodpile.

The Justice turned to the slave-catchers and told them that a card game with high stakes was about to begin and asked them if they would be interested in playing. Captain Throop assured the sheriff's men that he had no escaped slaves on board and the slave-catchers followed the Justice to the card game. Captain Throop stood on the deck of the *Ontario* stroking his Italian greyhound, Jeppa, as he called out "cast off." He smiled as his ship left the dock with another cargo of oppressed people headed for freedom.

It has been estimated that approximately 4,000 fugitive slaves traveled through Pultneyville to freedom in Canada. A third Underground Railroad station in the village was the "Selby House," located at 7851 Jay Street.

\* \* \*

## IMPRESSIONS OF A SEVEN-YEAR-OLD SLAVE

In the spring of 1825 in Maryland, a young slave was awakened by loud voices in the room next door. The seven-year-old boy could hear a man cursing and yelling and a woman begging for mercy. What he saw when he peeked through an opening in the boards of the wall between the two rooms remained with him for the rest of his life. He saw his fifteen-year-old aunt Hester, who had been stripped naked to the waist, standing on a stool. Her arms were over her head, her wrists were tied together, and the rope tying her wrists together had been hung on a hook in the ceiling joist.

The boy watched as his master, Captain Aaron Anthony, beat his aunt with a heavy, three-foot-long oxhide whip. The boy could hear the cracks of the whip across her tender back and the screams from the young woman interspersed with Anthony's curses. From the many blows, blood ran down the girl's back. Finally, Captain Anthony became exhausted and slumped to the floor.

The young boy was terrified by what he had seen. Later, he wrote, "I never shall forget it whilst I remember anything. It was the first of a long series of such outrages, of which I was doomed to be a witness and a participant. It struck me with awful force. It was the blood-stained gate, the entrance to the hell of slavery through which I was about to pass."

The incident was the boy's first experience of the cruelty of slavery and of the total domination of slaves by their master. The only crime committed by the boy's aunt Hester, a beautiful young woman, had been resisting the advances of her master.

The boy's name was Frederick Bailey, who later escaped from slavery and was known by the name of Frederick Douglass. He was a leading abolitionist and orator who edited the abolitionist newspaper, *North Star*, in Rochester. The self-educated Douglass became a reformer with an international reputation, a federal officeholder, and an advisor to Presidents. The impression made by his aunt Hester's beating never left him.

\* \* \*

## THE JERRY RESCUE

On October 1, 1851, the streets of Syracuse were crowded with visitors. Many abolitionists were visiting the city to attend the convention of the National Liberty Party, and other visitors had come for the Onondaga County Fair. Just as the convention delegates were finishing lunch, the bell of the Congregational Church began to peal. The Vigilance Committee recognized the signal that a fugitive was in danger. Other church bells began to ring, and soon the city buildings were emptied of their inhabitants.

Everyone headed for the office of Joseph F. Sabine, Commissioner of the United States Circuit Court, in the Townsend Block. William Henry, also known as Jerry McHenry, had been arrested by Deputy U.S. Marshal Henry W. Allen and accused of being a runaway slave.

Jerry was a forty-year-old African-American who worked at Frederic Morrell's cooper shop on North Salina Street. His mother was Celia, a slave who belonged to Mr. McReynolds of Buncombe County, North Carolina. Jerry, who was a red-headed mulatto, was thought to be the son of his master. Upon McReynold's death, his widow married William Henry, who gave Jerry his name. In 1818, William Henry moved with his family and his slaves to Hannibal, Missouri. Jerry escaped from his owner in Missouri in 1843 and moved to Syracuse in 1849.

Commissioner Sabine's office was surrounded by a large crowd. Before the charges could be read to Jerry, he ran away from his captors. He was shackled, but he outdistanced his pursuers for about a half mile down Water Street. When they caught him, he fought back and suffered a cracked rib and severe bruises. Edward Sheldon, founder of the Oswego Normal School, observed of Jerry's recapture, "I saw this fugitive from, not justice, but injustice, dragged through the streets like a dog, every rag of clothes stripped from his back, hauled upon a cart like a dead carcass, and driven away to a police office for a mock trial."

At the police station, which was then located between Water Street and the Erie Canal (now Erie Boulevard), Reverend Samuel May of the Unitarian Church calmed down the agitated captive by telling him that an escape was being planned. Reverend May then joined the Vigilance Committee who were meeting in Dr. Hiram Hoyt's office on South Warren Street. Meanwhile Marshal Allen, who was expecting trouble, called upon the Onondaga County Sheriff, William Gardner, for assistance.

Commissioner Sabine opened Jerry's hearing at 5:30 p.m. The large crowd gathered outside of the building continually interrupted the proceedings with yelling and rock-throwing. C. C. Foote, a National Liberty Party delegate from Michigan, spoke to the crowd in an attempt to calm them down. D. D. Hillis, Jerry's defense attorney tried to convince that crowd to go home because Jerry would be freed by the legal process. Samuel Ward, an African-American Congregational minister, also addressed the crowd, "We are witnessing such a sight as, I pray, we may never look upon again. A man in chains, in Syracuse! ... They say he is a slave. What a term to apply to an American! How does this sound beneath the pole of liberty and the flag of freedom?"

At dusk, the Vigilance Committee emerged from Dr. Hoyt's office, collected their clubs and a battering ram, and headed for the police station where Jerry was shouting that he would rather die than be returned to slavery. Ira Cobb turned off the gas lights, and the doors and all of the windows in the police station were smashed. Marshal Fitch from Rochester, who had joined Marshal Swift of Auburn and Marshal Bemis of Canandaigua in support of Marshal Allen, fired two shots, jumped thirteen feet out of a second story window, and broke his arm.

Jerry, who was too injured to walk, was carried to a waiting carriage and driven to the home of an African-American family, the Jacksons, where his shackles were removed. From there, he was moved to the home of a proslavery advocate, Caleb Davis, whose home on East Genesee Street was not likely to be searched. Jerry stayed with Davis for four days until his wounds healed, and then he was transported to Deacon Asa Beebe's barn in Mexico, Oswego County.

All vessels leaving New York for Canada were searched by U.S. marshals; it was difficult to make arrangements for Jerry's passage across Lake Ontario. Finally, the captain of an English cargo ship with a load of lumber agreed to provide passage for him. Orson Ames, owner of a sawmill and tannery in Mexico, shipped Jerry as a "consignment of boots and shoes" to Sidney Clarke in Oswego, who smuggled him aboard the cargo vessel.

Jerry arrived safely in Kingston, Ontario, and found a job in a furniture factory. He wrote to those who had helped him escape and thanked them for their help. He told them that he had "been led to think more than ever before of his indebtedness to God, and had been brought to the resolution to lead a purer, better life than he ever had done."

Not everyone agreed with the actions of the Vigilance Committee. Many citizens were concerned with the committee's taking the law into their own hands. The newspapers of Albany, Buffalo, Rochester, Syracuse, and Utica universally condemned the actions of the committee. Reverend Samuel May, a pacifist, favored open conflict when required to bring change. He wrote to New England Abolitionist William Lloyd Garrison, "I have seen that it was necessary to bring people into direct conflict with the Government—that the Government may be made to understand that it has transcended its limits—and must recede."

\* \* \*

# JOHN W. JONES OF ELMIRA

John W. Jones was born into slavery on the estate of the Elzy family of Leesburg, Virginia, on June 22, 1817. Jones's mother was born a slave, as was his father, who was sold by the Elzy family before Jones was born. Jones never saw his father. Miss Sally Elzy, a spinster and the owner of the estate, was a good mistress, and young Jones was her favorite. He worked around the house and garden until he was twelve, and then he worked in the fields.

When he was young, Jones saw a flock of Canadian geese flying northward in the early spring. He grandmother told him that they were flying to a region of the country where all people were free. This incident triggered his first thoughts of freedom. Eventually, Miss Elzy gave up the active management of the estate, and her health began to fail. It became obvious to Jones that Miss Elzy's heirs, whom he distrusted, would soon be in charge of the estate. He talked with his mother about turning his dreams of the North into reality.

In July 1844, Jones and five other slaves began their northern journey. They encountered many difficulties and had some narrow escapes along the way. They reached South Creek in Bradford County, Pennsylvania, which is located south of Elmira, without being captured. They stopped at the farm of Nathaniel Smith, crawled into the haymow in the barn, and fell into an exhausted sleep. Mrs. Smith discovered them, but she let them stay. She fed them three meals a day, and, slowly, they regained their strength.

After spending a week in the Smiths' barn, they walked to Elmira on the morning of July 5, 1844. Jones arrived in the city with $1.46 in his pocket; he earned fifty cents the first day splitting wood for Mrs. Culp, who was the daughter of Colonel John Hendy, a founder of Elmira. Jones attended public school in Elmira and in 1847 was appointed sexton of the First Baptist Church. When the local Underground Railroad was organized, Jones became an active member.

Elmira was a key station on the Underground Railroad. Passengers from Philadelphia were received in the city and sent either north to Ithaca or west via Corning and Bath. The refugees came in groups of six or seven, but on one occasion Jones housed thirty at one time in his small house next to the First Baptist Church. Many Elmirans provided financial assistance to the Underground Railroad movement, including Reverend Thomas Beecher, Jervis Langdon (Mark Twain's father-in-law), James Robinson, Riggs Watrous, and William Yates.

During the nine years that John W. Jones operated the Elmira station on the Underground Railroad, over 800 slaves were helped on their way to freedom. To Jones' knowledge, not one of them was captured and returned to the South.

\* \* \*

## Transported North in a L-Shaped Box

One day in the mid-nineteenth century, a businessman visited Attica, Wyoming County, west of the Finger Lakes Region, to transact business and stayed overnight. The next morning he met Colonel Charles O. Shepard, State Senator, member of the Liberty Party, and stockholder in the Underground Railroad. After breakfast, Shepard asked the businessman if he would like to see something unusual.

Shepard walked with him to a livery to show him a gardener's market wagon that had arrived in Attica a few days previously. It been used to transport a slave woman and her daughter from Washington, D.C. The women sat inside a box made of light boards. When viewed from the right side, the box was shaped like an "L." The back of the box was high, allowing the women to sit upright. The front of the box, which was low, fit under the driver's seat of the wagon. The women sat on the floor of the box and extended their feet under the seat of the wagon.

The wagon was driven from Washington, D.C., to Attica without a change of drivers or a change of horses. The women may not have had a comfortable ride, but they arrived across the Mason-Dixon line without being discovered.

\* \* \*

# People of the Underground Railroad

" 'Tis the law of God in the human soul,
        'Tis the law in the Word Divine;
It shall live while the earth in its course shall roll,
        It shall live in this soul of mine.
Let the law of the land forge its bonds of wrong,
        I shall help when the self-freed crave;
For the law in my soul, bright, beaming, and strong,
        Bids me succor the fleeing slave."

–Antislavery song

## LEVI COFFIN

*"If by doing my duty [aiding escaped slaves] and endeavoring to fill the injunctions of the Bible, I injured my business, then let my business go. As to my safety, my safety was in the hands of the Divine Master, and I felt that I had His approval. I had no fear of the danger that seemed to threaten my life or my business."*

*Levi Coffin*

Levi Coffin, the youngest of seven children, was born in 1798 in New Garden, North Carolina. His lifelong antislavery opinions were formed at age seven when he was with his father chopping wood on new Salisbury Road. He watched a coffle of slaves, handcuffed in pairs on each side of a long chain that extended between them, driven by a man on horseback with a long whip. Levi's father asked the slaves, "Well, boys, why do they chain you?" One of the slaves replied, "They have taken us away from our wives and children, and they chain us lest we should make our escape and go back to them."

Coffin asked his father many questions about the slaves that had just passed by them. Levi Coffin, Sr., described the institution of slavery to his young son without justifying it, because he couldn't. The thought that kept running through young Levi's mind was how he, his mother, and his sisters would feel if his father was taken from them.

A second incident of his boyhood impressed him with the injustice of slavery. Levi and his father went to the shad fishery at the narrows of the Tadkin River, where rapids were formed as the river flowed over a rocky bed through wild forest growth. The shad ascended the river each spring, and fishermen from all around the region came there to fish. The fishery was owned by the Crump brothers, who permitted their slaves to fish after the other fisherman were finished and to sell the fish that they caught after hours. Levi's father bought some fish from a slave the first night that they arrived.

The next morning the slave walked up to my father and asked if he would be interested in buying more fish that evening. One of the Crumps' nephews thought that the slave was being impertinent. The nephew picked a burning log from the fire and hit the slave a severe blow to the side of the head, baring his skull, covering his chest and back with blood, and setting his hair on fire.

Levi's father protested this brutality. Young Levi was unable to eat his breakfast that morning; he went off by himself and cried about "man's inhumanity to man." These were the first two instances that inspired Levi's hatred of slavery and made him resolve to do what he could to remedy the inequity between free people and slaves.

Coffin worked on the family farm until he was twenty-one, when he began teaching school. On October 28, 1824, he was married to Catherine White, a fellow member of the Religious Society of Friends (Quakers). Levi and Catherine grew up in the same neighborhood and had known each other since childhood. Catherine shared Coffin's interest in aiding the slaves, and she became an active supporter of the Underground Railroad.

In 1825, Coffin's parents and youngest sister moved to Indiana, where some of his married sisters lived. Coffin, Catherine, and their son, Jesse, followed them to Indiana in early 1826. Coffin opened a mercantile business in Newport, Indiana, which expanded during the twenty years that they lived there. In 1836, he added a linseed oil mill, but he was never too busy to participate in Underground Railroad activities.

Coffin was warned by friends that his Underground Railroad efforts put his life and his business interests at risk. He replied, "I told them that I felt no condemnation for anything that I had ever done for the fugitive slaves." Many of his proslavery customers left him, but new customers who moved into the area took their places.

Three Underground Railroad routes from the South converged at the Coffin house in Newport, Indiana: one from Cincinnati, one from Madison, and one from Jeffersonville, Indiana. Coffin had a team of horses and a wagon available at all times. Much of the expense of the Underground Railroad activity was paid for with earnings from his business. He and his wife would be awakened at any time of the night by knocks on the door alerting them to the arrival of new refugees with needs for food, clothing, and shelter.

Coffin received many threats because of his Underground Railroad activity. Proslavery supporters threatened to burn down his house, his store, and his pork-house. One letter, which was mailed from Kentucky, informed him that a gang of men was headed for

Newport to burn down the entire town. The townspeople went to bed and ignored the threat.

In the spring of 1847, Levi and Catherine Coffin moved to Cincinnati. Coffin knew many abolitionists in Cincinnati and had attended many of their meetings on his trips there. He wasn't sure how much Underground Railroad work he would do there; however, in a short period of time, he and Catherine were even busier than they had been in Indiana. They bought a large house in Cincinnati, which was suitable to their Underground Railroad activities. Refugees could be hidden in the upper rooms of the house for weeks, and boarders and visitors didn't know that they were there.

Underground Railroad activities were brisk in Cincinnati until the outbreak of the Civil War and for about a year afterwards, until slaves were received and protected inside of Union lines. With the ratification of the Fifteenth Amendment to the Constitution in 1870 stating that citizens shall not be denied the right to vote on account of race, color, or previous condition of servitude, Coffin was honored at a public gathering. The attendees paid tribute to Coffin for holding the position of president of the Underground Railroad for thirty years. At the conclusion of the meeting, he resigned his position and terminated the operations of the Underground Railroad.

Levi Coffin died at Avondale, near Cincinnati, on September 16, 1877. He had been in ill health for over a year. The Cincinnati *Daily Gazette* described his funeral service: "The funeral of Levi Coffin, the philanthropist, drew an overflowing audience to the Friends Meeting House ... Among the congregation were several of his surviving associates in anti-slavery work, his associates in the Freedman's Aid Commission, and dusky tear-bedewed faces of members of the once oppressed race, for whose emancipation he strove so long and earnestly."

The Reverend Dr. Rust, Secretary of the Freedman's Aid Society paid tribute to his friend's thorough unselfishness:

> He had too great a mission to perform to spare any time to take care of himself, and God took care of him. He was an honest, wise, and judicious man— wise in selecting the most practical and judicious methods. He was a brave and courageous man. It would take less bravery to go up to the cannon's

mouth than to do the work that he did. As he walked through the streets, he was hooted at and threatened by mobs. The battlefield has no such illustrations of heroism as as he exhibited every day. There is no American name more honored and revered in England than Levi Coffin. It is embalmed in the heart of every philanthropist in Britain. He has gone home.

The Reverend Rust wondered if the first to meet Levi Coffin on the other side were not hundreds and thousands of those men and women whom he had helped escape from bondage to freedom.

* * *

## FREDERICK DOUGLASS

*"It rekindled the few expiring embers of freedom, and revived within me a sense of my own manhood. It recalled the departed self-confidence, and inspired me again with a determination to be free.... He can only understand the deep satisfaction which I experienced, who has himself repelled by force the bloody arm of slavery. I felt as I never felt before. It was a glorious resurrection, from the tomb of slavery to the heaven of freedom. My long-crushed spirit rose, cowardice departed, bold defiance took its place, and I now resolved that, however long I might remain a slave in form, the day had passed forever when I could be a slave in fact."*

*Frederick Douglass*

Frederick was born in February 1818, in Talbot County, on the Eastern Shore of Maryland; he wasn't sure of the actual date of his birth. His mother, Harriet Bailey, was a slave and his father, whom he never met, was a white man. His master was Captain Aaron Anthony. In March, 1826, Frederick was sent to live with a member of Anthony's family, Hugh Auld, in Baltimore. Initially, Hugh's wife, Sophia, was kind to Frederick. He asked her to help him learn to read and write; she did so willingly until her husband heard what she was doing. Then the lessons stopped, and Sophia was no longer friendly to him. However, living in Baltimore was a good experience for him, and he had many opportunities to learn.

Thomas Auld, Frederick's legal owner, brought him back to rural slavery in 1833. Frederick did not like Auld or Auld's new wife, Rowena. He was not completely obedient, so Auld hired him out to Edward Covey, who had a reputation as a "slave-breaker." After Frederick had endured six months of flogging and other mistreatment, he turned on Covey in a two-hour fight that Frederick won. After that, Covey did not bother him, but Frederick was even more committed to winning his freedom. He began to help his fellow slaves with reading lessons.

In April, 1836, Frederick and five other slaves made plans to escape. However, one of the five told authorities of their plans, and they were jailed in Easton. Instead of selling Frederick, Thomas Auld sent him back to Hugh and Sophia in Baltimore. Frederick became an experienced caulker in a boatyard, where competition for jobs was fierce between poor white immigrants and slaves. Frederick was badly beaten because he was believed to have taken a job from a white immigrant.

Frederick continued his self-education with a membership in the East Baltimore Mental Improvement Society, a debating club. He met Anna Murray, a freed slave who was barely literate, at one of their meetings. They became engaged in 1838. They both saved money and made plans for an escape to the North. An argument with Hugh Auld motivated Frederick to board a northbound train and escape. The conductor asked to see his free slave papers, which he didn't have; Frederick showed him his seaman's papers instead. Despite some tense moments when he saw two local men who could identify him as a slave, he arrived in Philadelphia safely and then proceeded on to New York City.

Frederick stayed with David Ruggles, publisher of the antislavery quarterly, *The Mirror of Slavery*. He sent for Anna Murray, and they were married on September 15, 1838. Ruggles, who was active in the

Underground Railroad, suggested to Frederick and Anna that they move farther north. They moved to New Bedford, Massachusetts, where Frederick hoped to find work as a caulker. They lived with Nathan Johnson and his wife. Johnson suggested that since Frederick was an escaped slave, he should change his name. Johnson had just finished reading Sir Walter Scott's *Lady of the Lake;* he suggested the surname of "Douglass," the name of the Scottish lord and hero. Frederick Bailey became Frederick Douglass.

When Douglass looked for work as a caulker, he found that prejudice existed in the North as well as the South. The white caulkers didn't want to work with African-Americans. He was forced to take odd jobs as a common laborer. Anna helped by doing domestic work. One day he found a copy of William Lloyd Garrison's antislavery newspaper, *The Liberator,* and it changed his life. Garrison was a strong-willed abolitionist. In addition to being an editor, Garrison helped to found the New England Anti-Slavery Society. Douglass subscribed to Garrison's paper and was moved by it.

Douglass attended the annual meeting of the New England Anti-Slavery Society in New Bedford on August 9, 1841, and a meeting on the next day on the island of Nantucket. At the second meeting, Douglass was called upon to speak. Although he was nervous, he spoke movingly about his life as a slave and was well received. He was asked to become a full-time lecturer for the organization. He reluctantly accepted a three-month assignment and then stayed for four years. He improved his oratorical skills and became one of the Society's most popular lecturers.

The life of an abolitionist was not easy; Douglass had to learn to overcome hecklers. On September 15, 1843, he was severely beaten in Pendleton, Indiana. He escaped with a broken wrist and bruises. Abolitionist newspaper editor Elijah Lovejoy was killed in Alton, Illinois, while defending his press from an incensed mob. Another abolitionist, William Lloyd Garrison, was dragged through the streets of Boston with a rope around his waist and almost lost his life.

During the winter and early spring of 1844-45, Douglass took time off from the lecture circuit and wrote an autobiography, *The Narrative of the Life of Frederick Douglass, an American Slave.* In August of 1845, he went on a successful lecture tour of England, Ireland, and Scotland.

One month after Douglass' return to America, Anna and Ellen

Richardson of Newcastle raised money and negotiated for his freedom. They went through American agents to buy his freedom from the Aulds for $711.66. The deed of manumission was filed at the Baltimore Chattel Records Office on December 13, 1846, and Douglass was a free man.

He returned to England for another lecture tour in 1847. Upon his return to America, he proceeded with plans to publish an antislavery newspaper. His British friends raised $2,000 to help him get started. He was surprised when Garrison advised against it. Garrison, who did not want competition for his newspaper, *The Liberator*, said that there were already too many newspapers of that type.

Douglass started his newspaper in spite of Garrison's counsel against it. He knew that he would have to choose a base far from Garrison's in New England. Douglass chose Rochester, a booming city of 30,000 on the Erie Canal, where he had been well received on the lecture circuit in 1842 and 1847. The leading abolitionist of central New York, Gerrit Smith, supported him and gave him the deed to forty acres of land near Rochester. Douglass moved his family there on November 1, 1847.

On December 3, 1847, the first edition of his newspaper, *North Star*, was published. He named the paper *North Star* because the North Star was the guide that the slaves used when escaping from the South to freedom. In 1851, the *North Star* merged with the *Liberty Party Paper*, which was financed by Gerrit Smith; the resulting paper was called *Frederick Douglass' Paper*. In 1858, he began publishing *Douglass' Monthly* for British readers. The weekly ran until 1860, and he stopped printing the monthly in 1863, thus ending a sixteen-year publishing career.

Douglass served as a Rochester stationmaster on the Underground Railroad. He hid hundreds of escaping slaves at the *North Star* printing office, at his first house on Alexander Street just west of East Avenue, and at his later home on South Avenue near Highland Park. Douglass wrote about this effort:

> On one occasion I had at least eleven fugitives at the same time under my roof—until I could collect sufficient money to get them to Canada. It was the largest number at any one time and I had some difficulty in providing so many with food and shelter. But

they were content with very plain food and a strip of carpet on the floor for a bed or a place in the straw in the hayloft.

J. P. Morris was one of his main assistants in raising funds for the fugitives' escape. Douglass also received financial assistance from friends in England. William S. Falls, production foreman for the *Daily Democrat*, was another of his principal aides. He hid slaves in his press room, which was on another floor of the same building that housed Douglass' printing office. Falls also solicited money for Underground Railroad efforts from downtown Rochester business offices, such as the Reynolds Arcade.

Douglass also supported the Women's Rights Movement. On July 14, 1848, his *North Star* carried this announcement: "A convention to discuss the Social, Civil, and Religious Condition and Rights of Women will be held in the Wesleyan Chapel at Seneca Falls, New York, the 19th and 20th of July instant." The masthead that Douglas used for the *North Star* was: "RIGHT IS OF NO SEX–TRUTH IS OF NO COLOR."

In January, 1871, President Grant appointed Douglass to a commission to Santo Domingo (Dominican Republic). He moved to Washington. D.C., because he thought that more federal appointments would be offered. In 1877, President Rutherford Hayes appointed him United States Marshal for the District of Columbia. He served in that position until 1881, when President James Garfield appointed him Recorder of Deeds for the District of Columbia. He held that position until 1886.

Douglass' wife, Anna, died in August, 1882. In January, 1884, He married Helen Pitts, his secretary in the Office of the Recorder of Deeds. The mixed marriage caused controversy, but Helen said, "love came to me and I was not afraid to marry the man I loved because of his color." Douglass' response to critics was that his first wife "was the color of my mother and the second the color of my father."

In September 1889, President Benjamin Harrison appointed Douglass Minister-Resident and Consul-General to the Republic of Haiti, where he served until July 1891. Douglass, one of the strongest antislavery voices of his time, died of a heart attack in Washington, D. C., on February 20, 1895.

Pitt Homestead, Honeoye

\* \* \*

# THOMAS GARRETT

*"Judge, thou hast not left me a dollar, but I wish to say to thee, and to all in this courtroom, that if anyone knows a fugitive who wants a shelter and a friend, send him to Thomas Garrett, and he will befriend him."*

*Thomas Garrett*

Thomas Garrett, one of eleven children of Thomas and Sarah Price Garrett, was born in Upper Darby, Pennsylvania, on August 21, 1789. Thomas, Sr., operated mills and was a scythe- and tool-maker. Young Thomas worked in his father's businesses. The incident that motivated him to spent a lifetime supporting antislavery causes occurred when he was twenty-four years old and still living at home with his parents.

Garrett returned home one day to find his mother and sisters distressed. Two men had come to the house and kidnapped an African-American woman who worked for the family. He pursued their wagon, which was made easier to track by marks made by a broken wheel. He traced them to the Navy Yard and then to Kensington, where the men had stopped at a roadside tavern. He found the kidnapped woman in the kitchen of the tavern and returned with her to Upper Darby.

During the time he was pursuing the kidnappers and while riding home, Garrett thought about the wrongs of the slavery system. It was wrong that men thought that they had a right to enter a home and carry off a woman against her will. He made a resolution, at that time, to aid oppressed slaves in any way that he could.

On October 14, 1813, Garrett married Mary Sharpless of Birmingham, Pennsylvania, and in 1822 they moved to Wilmington, Delaware, which was a thriving town with plenty of opportunity for an ambitious young man. Garrett opened a iron, steel, and coal business on Shipley Street. He had early difficulties, which are described in William Still's book, *Underground Rail Road*:

91

> A rival house ... in the iron business, sought to run
> him off the track by reducing the price of iron to
> cost, but Friend Thomas, nothing daunted,
> employed a man to take his place in the store, tied
> on his leather apron, took to his hammer and anvil
> and in the prosecution of the trade learned from his
> father prepared to support his family with his own
> hands as long as the run lasted. Thus, by the sweat
> of his brow, he foiled the purpose of his rival and laid
> the foundation of what many reverses became one
> of the permanent business houses of the city.

Garrett had few close friends and was looked upon with suspicion; his house was under constant surveillance by the police, who realized that it was a station of the Underground Railroad. He was not bothered by his lack of popularity and adverse opinion because he knew that the Lord approved of his activities. Garrett said, "I believe in doing my duty. A man's duty is shown to him, and I believe in doing it, the first duty first and so on right along every time." His approach to life was summarized by Geoffrey Hubbard a century later, "Every Quaker defines his position fully and clearly by his life."

Garrett had a powerful physique and considerable personal bravery. He had no fear of the proslavery supporters who attempted to bully him. An example of his fearlessness was his response to a supporter of slavery who told him that if Garrett ever came to his town, he would shoot him. He responded, "Well, I think of going that way before long, and I will call upon thee." He called upon the man as he had promised. Garrett said, "How does thee do friend? Here I am, thee can shoot me if thee likes." He wasn't shot.

Men confronted Garrett flourishing pistols and bowie knives. He pushed them aside and told them that only cowards resorted to such measures. On one occasion, two men were overheard planning to kill him:

> He was warned, but having a meeting to attend that
> night, he went out as usual. In the street two men
> leaped upon him, but his brawny hands caught them
> by the backs of their necks and brought them up

standing. He shook them well and looked them over, then said, "I think you look hungry. Come in and I will give you supper." He forced them into his house and his wife prepared a warm supper, while Friend Thomas chaffed them about their adventure, and turned the enmity into friendship.

On another occasion, he boarded a train in Wilmington to pre-vent an African-American woman from being carried off to the South. Several southerners attempted unsuccessfully to throw him off the train. At one point, a reward of $10,000 was offered for him in Maryland. He wrote to the parties offering the reward and told them that this wasn't enough. For $20,000, he would go himself.

On July 13, 1828, Garrett's wife, Mary, died. She had been his partner in his Underground Railroad work. On January 7, 1830, he married Rachel Mendinhall, the daughter of a Quaker merchant who was a director of the National Bank of Delaware & Brandywine. Perhaps due to her ill health, Rachel appeared to stay in the back-ground and was not as active a participant as Mary had been in his antislavery activities.

In 1848, eight African-Americans—a man, his wife, and six chi-dren—ran away from a plantation on the eastern shore of Maryland. Except for two of the children that had been born in slavery, they were free. They sought refuge at the home of John Hunn, a wealthy Quaker, in Middletown, Delaware. Unfortunately, they had been fol-lowed. They were arrested and sent to jail in New Castle. The sher-iff and his daughter, who were antislavery supporters, notified Garrett of their plight.

Garrett visited them in jail in New Castle and returned to Wilmington. The following day, he and U.S. Senator Wales present-ed Judge Booth with a writ of habeas corpus. Judge Booth decided that there was no evidence to hold them, and, in the absence of evi-dence, "the presumption was always in favor of freedom." He dis-charged them. Garrett said, "Here is this woman with a babe at her breast, and the child suffering from a white swelling on its leg; is there any impropriety in my getting a carriage and helping them over to Wilmington?" Judge Boothe responded, "Certainly not."

Six weeks later, the slaveholders, Elizabeth Turner and Charles Glanding, filed a suit against Garrett in New Castle for helping fugitive slaves to escape. The trial, presided over by Judge Hall and Chief Justice Taney in May 1848, lasted three days. Garrett's friends suspected that the jury was packed against him. The verdict went against him, and every dollar of his property was taken from him. He responded, "Now, Judge, I do not think that I have always done my duty, being fearful of losing what little I possessed; but now that you have relieved me, I will go home and put another story on my house, so that I can accommodate more of God's poor."

His friends helped him in his time of difficulty. He was almost sixty years old, but he made the addition to his house and stepped up his support of the escaping slaves. His activities were aided by donations from friends in England. He continued to work to help the slaves until President Lincoln freed them in 1863 by signing the Emancipation Proclamation.

Thomas Garrett died on January 25, 1871. During his lifetime, he had helped just under 3,000 slaves on their travels to the North. Not one of these slaves was captured on the road to freedom. The exception was a slave who escaped, lived in Canada for a number of years, and returned to Wilmington to preach. He was seized and returned to bondage.

Throughout his life, Garrett lived his principles, "I should have done violence to my convictions of duty, had I not made use of all the lawful means in my power to liberate those people, and assist them to become men and women, rather than leave them in the condition of chattels personal."

\* \* \*

## GERRIT SMITH

*"[Slavery is] robbery, and the worst species of it—for it plunders its victim, not of goods and money, but of his body, his mind, his soul."*

*Gerrit Smith*

Gerrit Smith, the second youngest of the six children of Peter and Elizabeth Livingston Smith, was born on March 6, 1797, in Utica, New York. Peter was a partner of John Jacob Astor in the fur trade, and Elizabeth was a cousin of Robert Livingston, who as Chancellor of the State of New York, had adminstered the oath of office to President George Washington.

In 1806, Peter Smith moved his family to Peterboro in the town of Smithfield, Madison County. Gerrit worked on the family farm until 1814, when he entered Hamilton College at Clinton. On August 26, 1818, he graduated with highest honors and gave the valedictory address. In January 1818, Gerrit married Wealtha Ann Backus, daughter of the president of Hamilton College. Wealtha died of "dropsy of the brain" seven months after their wedding. Her grieving husband busied himself with his real estate purchases.

On November 1, 1819, Peter turned over the management of his vast real estate holdings to Gerrit and his uncle, Daniel Cady of Johnstown, who was the father of Elizabeth Cady Stanton of the Women's Rights Movement. Gerrit moved into the mansion house at Peterboro at that time. On January 3, 1822, Gerrit married Ann Carroll Fitzhugh of Rochester. The first children born of this congenial union were Elizabeth in 1822, Fitzhugh in 1824, and Ann in 1830.

In 1827, Smith purchased land from New York State on the east side of the river in Oswego at a public auction. He also invested in the Oswego Canal Company, which developed the water power of the Oswego River for industrial uses. The Oswego property became the largest source of his income, and the center of his business activity shifted to Oswego County from Madison County.

Smith relied on capable managers to run his land speculation interests, and then spent his time as he chose. Over the course of his lifetime, he wrote over 200 circular letters, speeches, and pamphlets on various political, social, and theological subjects in which he was interested.

In October, 1835, New York antislavery activists convened in Utica to form a state antislavery society. Conservatives broke up the meeting of 600 delegates held in the Second Presbyterian Church. Organized as the New York Anti-Slavery Society, the delegates reconvened at Temperance House and appointed Smith as chairman of a committee to schedule the next meeting. He scheduled the meeting for the following day at Peterboro, and 300-400 delegates attended.

Smith said to the delegates, "Resolved, that the right of free discussion, given to us by God, and asserted and guarded by the laws of the country, is a right so vital to man's freedom, dignity, and useful-ness, that we can never be guilty of its surrender, without consenting to exchange that freedom for slavery, and that dignity and usefulness for debasement and worthlessness."

Smith observed that free and open discussion was being threat-ened, not for a good purpose, but to support oppression; to ensure that "two millions and a half of our fellow men, crushed in the iron folds of slavery, may remain in all their suffering and debasement and despair." Furthermore, he commented that the suppression of free discussion at Utica verified what thinking people everywhere knew, "that slavery cannot live, unless the North be tongue-tied." On July 16, 1836, he was commissioned as a agent of the American Anti-Slavery Society and was expected to conduct meetings and establish auxiliary societies.

Smith was a agrarian whose wealth was principally in his land holdings. Believing that it was sinful to own more than one farm, he decided to give some of his 750,000 acres to 3,000 deserving African-Americans. He realized that there were needy white men, but one difference between them and blacks was that African-American men weren't allowed to vote. Most of the land that he gave away was in Essex and Franklin Counties in the Adirondacks. His version of land reform was not widely accepted, but he showed that he was willing to take action even if many viewed his action as misguided.

Smith also helped slaves to purchase their freedom. In 1836, he paid John Mason of Hagerstown, Maryland, $1,000 to liberate his slaves. Five years later, he paid S. Worthington of Mississippi $3,500 to free a slave family consisting of a husband, wife, and five children in. In 1846, Smith paid John Mason $1,000 for the manumission of ten slaves.

On another occasion, a newspaper reported that four slaves of the brother of John Mason ran away, stayed at Smith's home—the Peterboro Underground Railroad station, and were sent on their way to Canada. Mason read of their stay at Peterboro and wrote Smith questioning it. Mason asked why the slaves had left, because they were always well-treated. Smith replied that he merely gave them money, directions for their journey, and instruction in morals: "I obtained strong promises from the slaves, that they would totally abstain from intoxicating liquors, would be industrious, frugal, and virtuous...." Smith always invited the refugee slaves under his roof to family devotions and gave them advice on conducting themselves as free men.

In 1850, Smith ran for Congress from the twenty-second district, which included Madison and Oswego Counties. He ran as an independent candidate and beat both the Democrat and Republican candidates. He took his legislative responsibilities seriously; however, he knew that he would have to tread carefully. Abolitionists were not popular in Washington at that time.

In April 1854, Smith made a speech in Congress against the Kansas-Nebraska Bill, in which he disagreed in particular with the recognition of slavery in the territories. He had few close associates in Congress other than the abolitionist Senators Chase and Sumner. His isolation was a condition aggravated by the fact that he was not elected a member of either of the major parties. Increasingly, he felt frustration and futility in his role as a legislator. On August 7, 1854, he submitted his resignation before completing a full term.

Smith continued to support the Underground Railroad movement until the traffic in slaves tapered off with the outbreak of the Civil War in 1861. It became more difficult to travel in the South, and many slaves preferred to stay on the plantation until President Lincoln freed them. Smith ranked high among the reformers of his day. In 1872, he attended the Republican National Convention and received the greatest ovation of any delegate.

Modern historians, however, pay little attention to Smith. He made the speeches, wrote the propaganda, and provided the inspiration to keep the issues of the day before the public's eye. Perhaps if he had been a titan of industry or a career politician, his reputation might have been more long-lived. Obviously, his wealth played a large role in his ability to help the antislavery movement.

On December 28, 1874, Smith died, two days after suffering a stroke in New York City. Two obituaries provide a frame of reference for how highly he was regarded by his peers. The New York *Evening Mail* described him as:

> One of the greatest and best men who has been reared on American soil and has illustrated the value of American institutions. It has been a long, noble, and useful career—without a blemish on any part of it; one of sustained and natural dignity, one

that did not need the adventitious aid of high political stations. A mind more hospitable to new ideas, more thoroughly imbued with Democratic principles, more vigorous in the unselfish service of the race—has not been known in this country.

The New York *Times* concluded its three-column notice with:

The history of the most important half century of our national life will be imperfectly written if it fails to place Gerrit Smith in the front rank of men whose influence was most felt in the accomplishment of its results. Without official participation in politics beyond a single session in congress, he was active and powerful in forming the public sentiment that controlled politicians.

\* \* \*

## WILLIAM STILL

*"Where in history, modern or ancient, could be found a more Christlike exhibition of love and humanity, of whole-souled devotion to freedom, than was proven in the character of the hero, Seth Concklin, who lost his life while endeavoring to rescue from Alabama slavery the wife and children of [my brother] Peter Still."*

*William Still*

William Still, the eighteenth child of Levin and Charity Still, was born in Shamong, New Jersey, on October 7, 1821. Levin had been born into slavery on Maryland's Eastern Shore. He purchased his freedom from his master and moved to Burlington County, New Jersey. Charity escaped from her master in Maryland but was captured and returned to her owner. She was successful on her second attempt at gaining freedom and in joining Levin in New Jersey, but she had to leave her two oldest sons, Peter and Levin, in Maryland.

The family changed their name from Steel to Still, and Charity changed her name from Sidney to Charity to make it more difficult for the slave-catchers to find her.

Levin farmed, cut lumber, and raised chickens and pigs to eke out a living. The family sold fruit and vegetables at nearby markets. William did his share of chores on the farm and studied to educate himself, particularly in English, geography, and history. He was influenced by *The Young Man's Own Book* and by the antislavery newspaper, *The Colored American*. William left the family farm in the fall of 1841 to earn money to move to Philadelphia, where there were greater opportunities.

William moved to Philadelphia in the spring of 1844. He did odd jobs until he found work around the house and grounds of Mrs. E. Langdon Elwyn on West Penn Square. She allowed him to use her well-stocked library; he continued to educate himself. Mrs. Elwyn traveled widely and knew many of the leading public figures of the time. William was enlightened and fascinated by their conversations.

On Sundays, William worked at the Sunday school at the Moral Reform Retreat on Lombard Street. He met Letita George at church and found that they shared a common interest in helping the African-American people. In 1847, Letita and William were married.

William accepted a job as clerk and handyman for $3.00 a week working for James McKim at the Anti-Slavery office. Philadelphia, located just north of the Mason-Dixon Line, was a hub for slaves escaping to the North. Many Philadelphians, particularly the Quakers, were active in providing assistance to the fugitive slaves.

In 1833, the American Anti-Slavery Society was formed by William Lloyd Garrison, editor of Boston's abolitionist newspaper, *The Liberator*, and by other individuals who wanted to abolish slavery. The Pennsylvania Anti-Slavery Society was formed later that year. In 1840, James McKim became the corresponding secretary and general agent of that society and assumed the responsibility for publishing its newspaper, the *Pennsylvania Freeman*. With his new responsibilities, McKim became a key member of the Underground Railroad in Pennsylvania. Still became an active assistant to McKim in his efforts to help runaway slaves.

The December 9, 1852, issue of the *Pennsylvania Freeman* noted the strengthening of the Vigilance Committee that had grown out of the old Pennsylvania Society for the Abolition of Slavery. Still was appointed secretary of the committee whose purpose was to provide food, clothing, and shelter to fugitive slaves and to help them escape to Canada. Later, he was appointed chairman of the acting committee.

Still's duties included raising money to assist the runaways, advertising antislavery meetings, and printing handbills warning of slave-catcher activities. He read the notices of escaped slaves in the Baltimore *Sun* and the Richmond *Daily Dispatch* for information about runaways who would be arriving soon in Philadelphia. He kept a journal of the stories of the fugitives whom the Society assisted.

Still visited the communities in Canada, such as the Buxton Settlement and the Elgin Settlement, where the Vigilance Committee had sent escaped slaves. He was favorably impressed with the fugitives' life-style and work ethic. He noticed that those who were sufficiently motivated to escape tended to be energetic, industrious, and intelligent. He was assured that they were good citizens in their new environment.

In 1861, the Pennsylvania Anti-Slavery Society postponed their annual meeting due to the outbreak of the Civil War. The number of fugitives arriving in Philadelphia decreased because of the increased difficulties in traveling and because many of the slaves stayed on the plantations waiting for President Lincoln to free them. During the war years, Still, as a member of the executive committee of the Anti-Slavery Society, addressed the subject of equal rights for African-Americans. He originated a petition under the auspices of the Society's Social, Civil, and Statistical Association to obtain equality for them as railway passengers.

In January, 1863, the Emancipation Proclamation was signed, and the slaves were free. McKim reoriented the duties of the Anti-Slavery Society to helping the newly freed slaves. He offered Still the position of supplying food to the commissary of a camp of African-American soldiers. Still undertook these duties in addition to his lucrative coal business.

Because of his visibility in his efforts to obtain equality for railway passengers, some Philadelphia African-Americans were envious of Still's power and his financial success. They criticized him openly and even suggested not to buy coal from his Lehigh and Schuylkill Coal Company. His friends came to his defense:

> A Good Place to Get Coal— Mr. Wm. Still has now the finest coal-yard on Washington Avenue, fitted up by himself with an office, a stable, a car-track, and all the appurtenances and needs of a first-class coal depot. Everything seems to be constructed in the most substantial manner, wearing a neat, attractive appearance. His coal is of good quality and is furnished to dealers on liberal terms.

In 1871, an extended strike of coal miners gave Still the time to publish his journal of the activities of the Anti-Slavery Society in assisting escaping slaves. His monumental work, *The Underground Rail Road*, was published by Porter and Coates in 1872. It is one of principal sources of information about Underground Railroad activities.

Still joined the boards of various philanthropic organizations, such as the Home for Destitute Children and the Shelter, a home for children in Philadelphia. Also, he was elected a trustee of Storer College, a college for African-American students at Harper's Ferry, West Virginia.

Still contributed financially to the establishment of *The Nation*, a newspaper with commentary on art, literature, politics, and science, and in 1880 he helped to found a Y.M.C.A. for African-Americans in Philadelphia. On February 12, 1888, he became the first president of the Berean Building and Loan Association, a bank formed to provide home mortgages to African-Americans.

Still served as vice president of the Pennsylvania Anti-Slavery Society from 1887 to 1895. On December 26, 1895, he was elected president, and he served in that office until April 25, 1901, when his health began to fail. William Still died at his Philadelphia home on July 14, 1902. The New York *Times* referred to him as "the Father of the Underground Railroad." Over his lifetime, he had accumulated a estate worth between $750,000 and $1,000,000. However, his real accomplishment was the assistance that he provided to the thousands of members of his race in a time of need.

* * *

# HARRIET TUBMAN

*"When I found I had crossed that line, I looked at my hands to see if I was the same person. There was such glory over everything; the sun came like gold through the trees, and over the fields, and I felt like I was in heaven."*

*Harriet Tubman*

Harriet Ross Tubman, one of eleven children of Harriet Greene and Benjamin Ross, was born in 1820 on a plantation in Dorchester County on the Eastern Shore of Maryland. The plantation on Big Buckwater River, which was owned by Edward Brodas, was 100 miles south of the Mason-Dixon Line, sixty miles from Baltimore, and several miles from Bucktown. Harriet's parents were full-blooded Africans of the Ashanti, a West African warrior people.

Harriet, who was called Araminta at birth, was born in a slave cabin with an open fireplace and without windows or furniture. The family slept on the clay floor. When she was five years old, Harriet was hired out to a family named Cook. Mrs. Cook used Harriet to wind yarn. Because she was slow at the job, Harriet was turned over to Mr. Cook, who put her to work tending his muskrat traps. She waded in the cold water of the river with a thin dress and no shoes and eventually developed bronchitis and a high fever. Mr. Cook thought she was faking illness and returned her to her home plantation, where she recovered from bronchitis and a case of measles.

Harriet was hired out again, this time as a baby nurse and housekeeper. She said, "I was so little that I had to sit on the floor and have the baby put in my lap. And that baby was always on my lap except when it was asleep or when its mother was feeding it." When the baby awakened during the night, Harriet was expected to rock it in its cradle to prevent it from crying. If the baby's crying awoke Mrs. Cook, she would beat Harriet with a cowhide whip that left permanent scars on her back and neck.

Harriet was fed scraps from the table and was hungry most of the time. When she was seven, she took a lump of sugar from the sugar bowl. Mrs. Cook saw her take the sugar and got out her whip. Harriet fled the house and lived with the pigs in the pigpen for five days, competing with them for potato peelings and other scraps of food. Finally, she returned to the Cooks' home, where she was given a severe beating and sent home to the Brodas plantation.

Harriet was then hired out to split fence rails and load wagons with lumber. The heavy work was difficult for her, but she preferred it to being under the thumb of the mistress of the house. In her early teens, she worked as a field hand and saw many examples of cruelty to the slaves on the plantation. Later in life, she said of the owners and overseers, "They didn't know any better. It's the way they were brought up ... with the whip in their hand. Now it wasn't that way on all plantations. There were good masters and mistresses, as I've heard tell. But I didn't happen to come across any of them."

In 1835, when she was fifteen years old, Harriet saw a slave sneak away from the plantation. The tall African-American was followed by the overseer with his whip and by Harriet. The overseer soon caught the runaway slave and asked Harriet to hold the man while he tied him up. She refused. The black man ran away, and Harriet stood in the way to prevent pursuit. The overseer picked up a two-pound weight and threw it at Harriet. It struck her in the middle of her forehead, fractured her skull, caused profuse bleeding, and gave her a severe concussion.

Harriet was in a coma for weeks. For the rest of her life, she was affected by severe headaches and "sleeping fits," during which she would fall asleep for a few minutes—sometimes in the middle of a conversation. She was left with a depression in her forehead and a disfiguring scar. While she was in bed recovering, her master brought prospective owners to her bedside in attempts to sell her. No one wanted to buy her, even at the lowest price; she observed, "They said I wasn't worth a penny."

When Harriet had regained her strength, she was hired out to John Stewart, a local contractor. Initially, she worked as a maid in Stewart's home, but she begged him to let her work outdoors with the men. She cut wood, drove a team of oxen, and plowed. Soon she was swinging an ax to cut timber for the Baltimore shipbuilding industry. When work was slack on the Stewart farm, she was allowed to hire herself out to cut and haul wood for neighboring farmers. For this privilege, she paid Stewart fifty dollars a year and was permitted to keep anything she earned above that amount. In this way, she managed to put away a small nest egg.

While Harriet toiled at heavy outdoor work, she dreamed of being free. She thought, "I had reasoned this out in my mind; there was one of two things I had a right to, liberty or death; if I could not have one, I would have the other. For no man would take me alive; I should fight for my liberty as long as my strength lasted, and when it came time for me to go, the Lord would let them take me."

In 1844, Harriet married John Tubman, a free African-American who lived nearby. Tubman had been born free because his parents had been freed at their master's death. Her husband's freedom didn't change Harriet's slave status. Furthermore, her children would belong to the plantation. The constant threat to slaves in Maryland was to be "sold South," that is, sold to plantation owners from Alabama, Georgia, Louisiana, or Mississippi, where conditions for slaves were much harsher than in states closer to the Mason-Dixon Line.

One day Harriet heard that two of her sisters had been sold and were being transported south in chains. She knew of the Underground Railroad and of people who helped slaves escape. She didn't know geography, but she knew enough to follow the North Star to freedom. She tried to convince three of her brothers to come with her, but they were afraid of being captured and punished. She knew that her husband didn't want to travel to the North; in fact, he would have turned her in if he had known that she was leaving.

Harriet left the plantation in the middle of the night with some cornbread, salt herring, and her prized possession, a patchwork quilt. As she left, she sang an old spiritual:

> I'll meet you in the morning,
> When I reach the promised land,
> On the other side of Jordan.
> For I'm bound for the promised land.

Harriet went to the house of a woman who was known to help slaves escape. The woman took her in and gave her a slip of paper noting her next stop on the way to freedom. Harriet was so grateful that she gave the woman her quilt. She was tired when she arrived at the next stop early in the morning. The woman opened the door and handed her a broom and told her to start sweeping the yard. At first, Harriet was suspicious; then she realized that no one would question a slave working around the house. The woman's husband put her in his wagon, covered her with vegetables, and took her to the next stop that evening, generally following the course of the Choptank River.

Harriet finally crossed the Mason-Dixon Line and entered Pennsylvania. She was free, but she didn't have any contacts to help her find a job and a place to live. In her words, "I was a stranger in a strange land."

Harriet made her way to Philadelphia, where she found a job in a hotel kitchen cooking and washing dishes. She met two of the founders of the Philadelphia Vigilance Committee, James Miller McKim, a white clergyman, and William Still, a freeborn African-American. They needed someone to guide a slave family north from Cambridge, Maryland. Harriet volunteered, but they hesitated letting her go because she might be retained in the South as a slave. When she found out that the family was her sister, Mary, and her brother-in-law, John Bowley, she insisted on going. She brought them to safety in Philadelphia.

In the spring of 1851, Harriet made her second trip south to guide fellow slaves northward. This time she guided her brother, James, and two of his friends to freedom. The overseer and the hounds were on their trail. Harriet evaded the dogs by crossing an ice-cold river. None of them could swim, and the men resisted the crossing. She waded out into swift-flowing water up to her chin to prove that they could make it across. If she hadn't changed their route on a hunch, they would have been captured.

On her next trip to Dorchester County, Maryland, she stopped at her husband's cabin. She found that he had remarried and had no interest in traveling north. She brought several slaves back to Philadelphia, being very careful in country in which she was known.

The route northward that Harriet used was through Delaware, waiting until the last moment to cross into Maryland. One reason was that Delaware was the site of the headwaters of many of the rivers that drained through the Eastern Shore into Chesapeake Bay. Secondly, the state's African-American population in 1860 contained only 1,798 slaves out of a total of 21,627. Delaware was the only southern state in which an African-American was assumed to be free until proved to be a slave.

When she approached a stop on the Underground Railroad, Tubman would hide her "passengers" before she rapped on the door. Then she would announce that she was "a friend with friends." Many of her trips north were via Wilmington, Delaware, the home of Thomas Garrett, a leader of the Underground Railroad movement.

Garrett, a Quaker who became a good friend of Harriet's, helped over 2,700 slaves to escape. He was fined, jailed, and sued, but nothing deterred Garrett form helping those less fortunate than he was— not even the loss of his personal fortune and his business. William Lloyd Garrison, the Boston abolitionist leader, considered Garrett to be "one of the best men who ever walked the earth."

On September 18, 1850, the passage of the Fugitive Slave Act made helping escaped slaves riskier. United States marshals were empowered to catch runaways and return them to their owners. Anyone assisting a fugitive could be fined $1,000 and sent to jail. Slave-catchers were hired to pursue runaway slaves who had thought that they were safe in the North. More slaves were now going to Canada, which was beyond the reach of the Fugitive Slave Act and the slave-catchers. Harriet said, "I wouldn't trust Uncle Sam with my people no longer." Eventually, she moved from Philadelphia to St. Catherines, Ontario, where she lived for five years.

In December 1851, Harriet made her fourth trip south. On her return, she guided another one of her brothers and his wife to freedom. When she reached Garrett's home in Wilmington, she added nine more passengers, including a baby. From this trip onward, she carried a sedative to keep baby passengers quiet. Between 1851 and 1857, Harriet made a spring trip and a fall trip to Maryland's Eastern Shore each year. On these trips, she met many of the leaders of the Underground Railroad movement, including John Brown, Frederick Douglass, J. W. Loguen, and Gerrit Smith. Brown called Harriet "General Tubman."

On one of her trips, Harriet had a nervous passenger who panicked and wanted to turn back. Harriet knew that he would be tortured to describe escape methods and "stations" on the road north. She pointed a gun at his head and told him to keep walking, while reminding him that if he were dead he couldn't reveal any information. Such an event occurred more than once on her trips on the Underground Railroad.

Harriet frequently stopped at Cooper House in Camden, Delaware, and hid her passengers in a secret room above the kitchen. In Odessa, Delaware, they hid in a concealed loft over the sanctuary in a Quaker meeting house. On many farms, the slaves hid in a "potato hole," a rough vegetable cellar with few amenities. On one occasion Harriet pretended to be reading a book when the slave-catchers passed by. One of the men said to the other, "This can't be the woman. The one we want can't read or write."

People began to call Harriet "the Moses of her people." A $12,000 reward was offered for her capture. She made her last journey on the railroad in 1860. In nineteen trips, she led over 300 slaves to their freedom. During the Civil War, she worked with slaves who had been left behind when their owners joined the Confederate Army.

Major General David Hunter was pleased to have Harriet's help with the slaves at Beaufort, South Carolina. She also served as a nurse at Hilton Head, South Carolina, and in Florida. For three years of service to the federal government, she was paid only $200, most of which was used to build a washhouse where she instructed the slave women in doing laundry to support themselves.

During the summer of 1863, Harriet worked as a scout for Colonel James Montgomery, who commanded an African-American regiment. Harriet assembled a network of spies, who notified her which slaves were ready to leave their masters and serve in the Union Army. She was supposed to receive a reward for recruiting slaves to the Grand Army of the Republic. She was owed at least $1,800 for her efforts, but she was never paid.

In 1864, Harriet was exhausted, and her seizures were occurring more frequently. She went to Auburn, New York, to rest and recuperate. While in Auburn, she heard that her husband, John Tubman, had died. In 1867, Harriet's friend, Sarah Bradford, wrote a biography about her and turned over the proceeds of the book, $1,200, to her. Some of the money went to African-Americans who needed food and clothing.

On March 18, 1869, she married Nelson Davis, whom she had met in South Carolina during the war. William H. Seward, Secretary of State in the Lincoln and Johnson administrations, attended her wedding. Seward had obtained some property for Harriet when she first moved to Auburn; they maintained their friendship until he died in 1872.

In 1888, Harriet puchased a 25-acre property at a public auction to establish a home for African-Americans who were ill and needy. She lacked the money to build the home, so she deeded the property to the African Methodist Episcopal Zion Church. The church built the home, but Harriet was unhappy when she heard that it cost $100 to enter it.

Harriet's second husband died in 1888. In 1890, Congress approved pensions for widows of Civil War veterans. Since Davis had served in the Union Army, she was entitled to eight dollars a month, which was increased to twenty dollars a month in 1899. This was the only money she received from the government; she was never paid for her efforts during the Civil War.

On March 10, 1913, Harriet died of pneumonia at the age of ninety-three, after living two years in the home that she had helped to establish. The Auburn post of the Grand Army of the Republic gave her a military funeral, at which Booker T. Washington spoke. Harriet was truly the Moses of her people; she was also an abolitionist, a humanitarian, a nurse, and a spy. Today, she is most widely remembered for her Underground Railroad activities, about which she said, "I never ran my train off the track, and I never lost a passenger."

# Routes Through the Finger Lakes Region

*"Then lift that manly right hand, bold ploughman of the wave. Its branded palm shall prophesy, 'Salvation of the Slave.'"*

—John Greenleaf Whittier

Many of the escaped slaves traveled through Wilmington, Delaware, where they were aided by Thomas Garrett, a Quaker and a strong abolitionist. From Wilmington, most of the fugitives were transported to Philadelphia, where they were clothed and helped by William Still, a free African-American. Many of the fugitives traveled to Elmira, New York, where they were routed either to Ithaca, Watkins Glen, or Bath via Corning. From Bath they were transported across western New York to Lewiston and Canada. Another route from Philadelphia was via the Susquehanna Valley to Athens, Pennsylvania, where they crossed the state line into Waverly, Owego, and Binghamton and then either to Syracuse or to Albany on their journey northward.

At least five routes went north from Ithaca: along the west shore of Cayuga Lake, by boat via the lake to the village of Cayuga on the eastern shore, along the eastern shore of Cayuga Lake, north to Auburn, and northeast through Cortland to Syracuse. From Syracuse, the slaves were moved to Oswego, where they were transported across Lake Ontario to Canada. Gerrit Smith, one of the strongest supporters of the Underground Railroad movement lived in Peterboro, Madison County, east of Syracuse. His home, which was destroyed by fire in the 1930s, was an Underground Railroad station.

From Corning, the slaves either went north via Hornby to Watkins Glen and along either the west or east side of Seneca Lake to Geneva, or they traveled to Bath and then to Canandaigua, either via Branchport along the western shore of Keuka Lake or to Naples and then north along Canandaigua Lake's West Lake Road.

Much Underground Railroad traffic moved along the road that is now Routes 5 and 20 at the northern end of the major Finger Lakes. The slaves traveled east from Auburn to Syracuse or west from Auburn to Rochester. Much of the Rochester traffic had a destination of St. Catherines, Ontario. Slaves went across Lake Ontario by ship from Pultneyville or Rochester to locations in Canada and from Oswego to Kingston, Ontario.

Over forty Underground Railroad stations are still standing along the following eight routes through the Finger Lakes Region of New York State indicated on the maps of the region. Except for a few churches, a restaurant, and a museum, most of these homes are private residences. When following these routes, respect the owners' right of privacy. The owners of those houses that have a state historical marker in front are used to visitors looking at and taking pictures of their home. Those homeowners who do not have a marker are not as used to visitors. Give them the consideration that you would like to receive if you lived there.

# Authentication of Underground Railroad Stations

It is difficult to verify that a house was actually an Underground Railroad station. Two factors that contribute to this difficulty are that the activities occurred over a century and a half ago and that aiding fugitive slaves was against the laws of the time. Obviously, owners didn't want it known that their home was a station on the Underground Railroad. Severe fines were levied for anyone caught aiding or harboring escaped slaves. Over forty Underground Railroad stations are still standing along the following eight routes through the Finger Lakes Region of New York State indicated on the sectional maps of the Region.

Information on the Underground Railroad stations along these eight routes is available from open, public sources. All of the information provided in this book is from secondary sources: books, magazines, newspapers, historical society articles, and reference material in area libraries.

None of the information is from primary sources, e.g. from interviews of the current owners of the houses or relatives of the family that was active in the Underground Railroad. In researching the Underground Railroad stations, verbal information was received from individuals but not used because of the difficulty of distinguishing fact from speculation. All of the information in the book on Underground Railroad stations is from written reference material, which in many cases, but not all cases, was verified by historical society personnel.

Obviously, some of the information is easy to verify. If there is a New York State historical marker in front of the house identifying it as an Underground Railroad station, it is highly probable that it was. If county, town, and village historians state that a house was a station, it probably was. However, the mere identification of a house as a station in a book, magazine, newspaper, or in reference material in a local library does not necessarily authenticate that it was, in fact, a station.

In this book, the stations are grouped into three categories: those verified by a New York State historical marker, those authenticated

111

by a historical organization, and those mentioned in written reference material but not necessarily verifiable as a station. In a sense, it is equally difficult to verify that a house wasn't a station on the Underground Railroad as it is to prove that it was.

**Examples of houses in the first category with NYS historical markers are:**

- Edwards House, Fruit Valley (Oswego)

- Hanford House, Etna

- Ferry Farm, Seneca Falls (Bridgeport)

- Pliny Sexton house, Palmyra

- Salisbury-Pratt House, Little York

- Warrant Homestead, Brighton

**Houses in the second category, those verified by historical organizations, include:**

- Cooper Farmhouse, Cortland

- Evergreen House, Skaneateles

- Hargous-Briggs House, Pittsford

- John W. Jones House, Elmira

- McBurney House, Canisteo

- Parker-Wixom House, Mecklenburg

- Pitt Homestead, Honeoye

- Uncle Billy Marks Funeral Home, Naples

- Wesleyan Methodist Church, Columbus Circle, Syracuse

Examples of houses in the third category, identified in written reference material, are:

- 125 Washington Street, Bath
- 351 Front Street, Owego
- 5821 Route 21, Williamson
- Esperanza, near Branchport
- Fairview Manor, Big Flats
- Greystone Inn, Lansing
- Maxfield Inn Carriage House, Naples
- Perkins House, Athens, Pennsylvania
- Van Houten House, Geneva

Route I. East to West along Routes 5 and 20 from Syracuse to Rochester

# I. EAST TO WEST ALONG ROUTES 5 AND 20 FROM SYRACUSE TO ROCHESTER

**1. Syracuse, 304 E. Onondaga Street (overlooking Columbus Circle)**—The Wesleyan Methodist Church is one of the last remaining Underground Railroad stations in Syracuse. In a one-month period in the early 1850s, church member Luther Lee helped thirty-four fugitive slaves to escape. The church is also one of the few survivors of the many Syracuse churches and buildings where abolitionist meetings were held. The Wesleyan Methodist Church broke from the Methodist Church in the early 1840s over the issue of slavery. Construction of the red brick church was completed in 1846. The brick tower at the west entrance and the two-story structure at the east side of the church were completed in 1858. In 1878, a spire was added to the tower.

Seven sculptures have been carved into clay in the wall of the fifty-foot-long basement of the church. It is believed that they were carved by fugitive slaves who were hiding in the church on their route to Canada and freedom. Only one of the seven unfired-clay faces remains in its original form without substantial deterioration; however, the nose on the face is chipped. The hair is parted on one side in page style, and there are no pupils in the almond-shaped eyes. A member of an archaeological team from Syracuse University interprets the face as a composite of two people—abolitionist leaders Frederick Douglass, who spoke in the church, and the Reverend Jermain Loguen of Syracuse.

Dating by archaelogists of Underground Railroad activity is based on a fragment found in the basement cavern of a black-transfer print dish, which was a style of whiteware used from 1830 to 1850. The church is listed in the National Register of Historic Places.

**2. Skaneateles, 98 W. Genesee Street**—"Evergreen House" is the only verifiable Underground Railroad station still standing in Skaneateles. The house was built by James Canning Fuller, a Quaker who arrived in Skaneateles from England on April 20, 1834. Fuller was a strong abolitionist who gave many speeches on the subject of the immorality of slavery. Mr. and Mrs. Fuller traveled to the South to buy slaves, whom they released when they arrived back in the North.

Evergreen House, Skaneateles

The Reverend Jermain Wesley Loguen, who was active in the Underground Railroad movement in Syracuse, stayed with the Fullers for several days enroute to escaping to Canada.

After his death on November 25, 1847, Fuller's widow continued to use the house as an Underground Railroad station. Their son was an active member of the Anti-Slavery Society in Syracuse. Mrs. Fuller sold the home to James A. Root, an abolitionist who continued to operate the house as a station on the Underground Railroad.

The T-shaped Evergreen House has three columns and a porch and second-story veranda at its eastern entrance. No hiding places used by escaped slaves have been found in the house.

3. **Auburn, 33 South Street**—The "Seward Mansion" was built in 1816-17 by Judge Elijah Miller, William H. Seward's father-in-law. The federal-style mansion, a registered National Historic Landmark, was expanded in 1847 and in 1860. All rooms in the 30-room house, half of which are open to the public, are furnished only with original family pieces and gifts and memorabilia collected in Seward's travels.

The parlor of Seward House contains the gilded furniture, upholstered with its original tapestry material, from the parlor of Seward's Washington home when he was Secretary of State in Abraham Lincoln's and Andrew Johnson's administrations. The fireplace mantel in the parlor was built by a sixteen-year-old journeyman painter and carpenter, Brigham Young, who inherited the leadership of the Mormon Church from its founder, Joseph Smith.

Guests who were served in the dining room included Presidents John Quincy Adams, Martin Van Buren, Andrew Johnson, and William McKinley. Other luminaries who dined there were Henry Clay, General Custer, Admiral Farragut, General Grant, and Daniel Webster.

Fugitive slaves who stopped at Seward House on their journey to freedom stayed in one large room and one small room on the second floor in the back of the mansion. They entered and left via a stairway off a passageway leading to the courtyard just around the corner from the kitchen. The two beautiful stone outbuildings, or carriage houses, in back of the mansion, were not used to hide escaped slaves. In the first half of the nineteenth century, the property was an operating farm. One of the stone carriage houses behind the mansion was a stable, and farm tools were stored in the other.

Ferry Farm, Seneca Falls (Bridgeport)

**4. Seneca Falls, Lower Lake Road (Bridgeport)**—The picturesque two-story cobblestone home has a historical marker in the front yard containing the words: "The Cobblestone or Ferry Farm—known during the Civil War as a station on the so-called underground railway. The trail of slaves to Canada was broken by bringing them across the lake from Union Springs, which was a ardent abolition Quaker village. This too was the landing place of an Indian canoe ferry and of the first white man's ferry." Ferry Farm, which faces Cayuga Lake, is located in the hamlet of Bridgeport.

**5. Geneva, 20 Pulteney Street**—The "Van Houten House" is a two-story frame house with a one-story addition on its south side. When the house was remodeled years ago a bullet hole was found in the front door. Men chasing an escaped slave fired the shot through the door. Just before they arrived, grandmother Van Houten, a spirited woman and a devout Methodist, heard shouting and saw an African-American running up the sidewalk toward the house. She let the escaped slave in and bolted the door. She gave him part of a loaf of bread, guided him out of the back door, and told him to rattle the back fence to let her know that he had escaped. She opened the door to the boisterous men and invited them to search her home. While they were searching the second floor, she heard the back fence being rattled.

**6. Canandaigua, 3402 W. Lake Road**—The "Cobblestone Farm" was built by Isaac Parrish in 1837. The beautiful two-story cobblestone house was a station on the Underground Railroad when owned by Isaac Parrish and after it was purchased by Robert and Maggie Gorham Benedict in 1858. Escaped slaves were transported to Cobblestone Farm from Naples by William ("Uncle Billy") Marks, Jr., in one of his mortuary's horse-drawn hearses.

The fugitives were hidden in a secret room in the attic adjacent to the south wall of Cobblestone Farm. The fleeing slaves were led up to the attic where they walked on loose floorboards around the south chimney through a doorway into a small room, which was six feet wide and ten feet long. The ceiling was five feet, four inches high at the peak sloping down to four feet where the ceiling joined the walls. The back wall is stone and mortar, and the walls are plaster. The room would have been stifling hot in the summer—it had no

Cobblestone Farm, Canandaigua

windows—and bitter cold in the winter.

**7. Canandaigua, 104 Gibson Street**—The graceful two-story frame house with a mansard roof and detailed ornamental trim was a station on the Underground Railroad on routes both to Rochester and to Pultneyville. In emergencies, slaves descended through a trap door in the dining room to a dry cistern in the basement. The trap-door was near the north wall of the dining room and was covered by the dining room table. Most of the escaped slaves arrived in Canandaigua either from Naples or from Geneva on their way to Canada.

**8. Perinton, 173 Mason Road** (north of the village of Egypt)—The sprawling two-story frame house was built in 1816 by Gilbert Ramsdell, a Quaker and an abolitionist. Ramsdell moved to Perinton from New England with his father while he was still a young man. He taught school in Macedon and saved his money to build the house that replaced the family log cabin, the first structure on the property. He built the large house for his bride, Harriet Smith, who joined the Society of Friends when they were married.

Large boulders were used to construct the cellar walls; wrought iron nails were used in the lumber cut on the site to build the original house, which had high ceilings in its many rooms. The home was so large and so unusual that it was called "Ramsdell's Castle."

**9. Perinton, 2187 E. Whitney Road**—This two-story frame house was used by John Tallman as a station on the underground railroad. His son, John, Jr., presented to a historical society a paper in which he commented:

> In 1859-60 a runaway slave from Georgia, his wife and a half a dozen children were concealed in our house for a week on their way to Canada. They were quartered in the kitchen and were provided with food ... sufficient for several days.... [My] father in the dead of night packed the family in a lumber wagon under quilts and blankets and drove them to the next station.

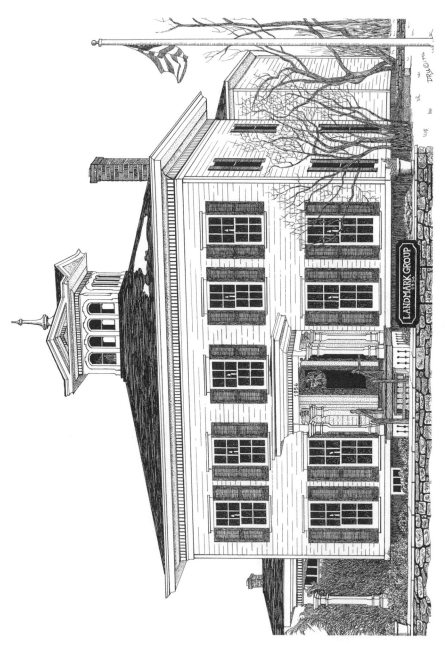

Warrant Homestead, Brighton

The next station was in Rochester along the way either to a boat across Lake Ontario to Canada or west from Rochester via Buffalo to St. Catherines, Ontario.

**10. Brighton, 1956 W. Henrietta Road**—The "Warrant Homestead" replaced a log cabin built on the site in 1819 by Thomas Warrant. Warrant moved to Rochester in 1818 from Yarmouth, England, by way of Canada. He was a coppersmith who had to smuggle his tools across the U.S./Canadian border because of existing laws.

Warrant was a Baptist and a staunch abolitionist. He hid escaping slaves in his barns across the road from his L-shaped brick house and in the upper rooms at the back. His barns and the back door of his home were never locked. The fugitive slaves climbed the back stairway, which was heated by woodburning stoves, to their rooms. When it was safe to move them, he transported the slaves under hay in his wagon to Underground Railroad stations along the shore of Lake Ontario for passage to Canada.

The Warrant Homestead was enlarged at the time of the Civil War, the original brick was covered with clapboards, and a cupola was added to the roofline. A historic marker outside of the house bears the words: "Warrant Homestead. Settled in 1819 by Thomas Warrant, a coppersmith and abolitionist. This home was used as a station of the Underground Railroad."

One route to Rochester from Canandaigua went through Victor, Perinton, and Pittsford; another route went through East Bloomfield, Ionia, Mendon, Henrietta, and Brighton. A third route proceeded westward from Palmyra through Macedon, Egypt, and Perinton. From Rochester, refugees either traveled west along Ridge Road to St. Catherines and other Ontario communities or boarded ships to cross Lake Ontario to Toronto and other Canadian cities.

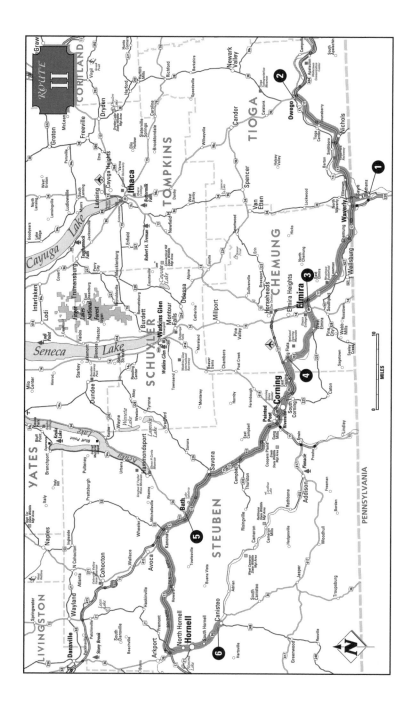

Route II. East to West along Route 17 from Owego via Elmira to Bath and West

## II. East to west along Route 17 from Owego via Elmira to Bath and west

A major route north from Philadelphia was via the Susquehanna Valley to Athens, Pennsylvania, and then either west to Elmira or east to Owego and north to Ithaca via Danby. Escaped slaves who traveled west from Elmira went to Bath via Big Flats, Corning and Painted Post. An alternate route went north from Corning via Hornby to Watkins Glen.

1.   **Athens, Pennsylvania, 729 Main Street**—The "Perkins Home" is a two-story frame house built in 1827 by pharmacist George Perkins, was a temporary stopover for escaped slaves who were traveling north from Philadelphia via many intermediate stations. The fugitives knocked on the ground-level door at the rear of the house after dark, and Perkins gave them food and a candle and hid them in the stone cellar. He told them that he would pound on the floor to warn them to hide in the hiding place if strangers came to the door.

The fugitives were hidden in the basement in an ash pit below the two fireplaces on the first floor. Stones had been removed to expand the "hidey hole" to four and a half feet wide, eight feet long, and six and a half feet high. It was large enough to accommodate four to six refugees and is still there today. The slaves  slid through a narrow ground-level hole in a stone wall that provided access to a small room with a floor area of six feet by eight feet. They could stand in the hiding place and look up through the chimney to see the sky on a moonlit night. A flue in the chimney provided them with fresh air.

2.   **Owego, 351 Front Street**—The two-story frame house was built between 1806 and 1809, and is the oldest home in the village. Prior to the Civil War, the home was owned by Judge Farrington, who was a stationmaster on the Underground Railroad. Escaped slaves were transported from Athens, Pennsylvania, and then either west to Elmira or east via Owego to Binghamton and  to Syracuse or Albany.

In later years, when a storeroom in the house was remodeled into a bedroom, the owners discovered a steep staircase that led to a small door in the attic. The door required one to stoop to pass through it into the small room where the slaves where hidden.

Refugee slaves were also temporarily hidden in a bricked-up

351 Front Street, Owego

space in the basement that was only four feet wide and four feet deep. An owner discovered the hiding place when the floorboards that had been covered with earth rotted out, and he fell into the hole.

3. **Elmira, 311 Woodlawn Avenue**—The small one-story bungalow, which is apparently the only Underground Railroad station still standing in Elmira, was the home of John W. Jones, an ex-slave. The house, originally located on a sixteen-acre farm at 1259 College Avenue, was rotated ninety degrees when it was placed on a basement constructed for it at its present site. Jones, who was born into slavery in 1817 on a plantation in Leesburg, Virginia, escaped to the North in June 1844.

In 1847, he was appointed sexton of the First Baptist Church in Elmira and in 1851 became an active stationmaster on the Underground Railroad. During his nine years as a stationmaster, he helped over 800 fugitive slaves to escape, usually in parties of six or seven. To his knowledge, none of them was caught. Elmira was a principal hub on the Underground Railroad. It received many slaves sent northward by William Still of Philadelphia.

4. **Big Flats, Route 352**—"Fairview Manor," located just east of Smithome Farm, was built in 1812 by Clark Winans. The bricks, which were fired on the property, used to build Fairview Manor were laid three deep to form the exterior walls and were used in the four chimneys. Some of the material used to construct the house, such as glass for the "twelve over eight" windows, the Norfolk iron latches, and the staircase that is the focal point of the central hall, was shipped in from outside the area.

A large, flat piece of fieldstone in the base of the fireplace was removable, providing an entrance into an underground cave dug just outside of the foundation. Escaping slaves would be led into the underground room, the fieldstone base for the fireplace would be put back in place, and a fire would be started in the fireplace. When it was time for the slaves to move onto the next station on the Underground Railroad, the fire was extinguished, and the slaves were brought up through the cooling fireplace.

It is rumored that a half-mile-long tunnel was built from the basement of Fairview Manor to the Chemung River to help slaves escape. This is unlikely, since the overflowing river would flood the

Fairview Manor, Big Flats

basement each spring.

In the late 1800s, the family who owned the house harbored a band of counterfeiters who set up their printing press in the secret room in the basement. The counterfeiters moved on just before the federal agents raided the site. They re-established their printing operation on an island in the Chemung River.

**5. Bath, 125 Washington Street**—The small two-story frame house on the south side of Washington Street was a station on the Underground Railroad that received refugee slaves from Elmira, Big Flats, and the Corning area. In emergencies, the slaves were hidden in a fruit cellar in the basement. From this station, escaped slaves were transported to Naples or to Penn Yan on their way north.

**6. Canisteo, McBurney Road**—The two-story, frame "McBurney House," which was built by Colonel James McBurney in 1797, is the oldest house in Steuben County. McBurney was a peddler who moved to the area from Pennsylvania and acquired 1,600 acres of land. The house has seventeen rooms, many of which are large, including a thirty-foot-long ballroom on the third floor. The roof is supported by foot-square beams, and a large clay and stone fireplace is located at one end of the attic. The other two fireplaces are under this one on the first two floors.

The slave quarters were located in the part of the house north of the main structure. The slaves' kitchen had a fireplace ten feet wide with baking and warming ovens equipped with andirons, hooks, tongs, and a swing crane. Sleeping rooms for the slaves were above the kitchen. An addition that was torn down in 1940 provided quarters for more slaves. Just prior to the Civil War, the family of Thomas McGee, a nephew of Colonel McBurney, owned the house and operated it as a station on the Underground Railroad. Subsequent owners of the house remembered a tunnel that ran from the chicken house behind the main house to the nearby riverbank. The chicken house has been torn down and the tunnel filled in; however, musket balls are still imbeded in the front door, causing much speculation.

From Canisteo, most fugitives traveled west through Allegany County or north via Hornell, Arkport, and Dansville.

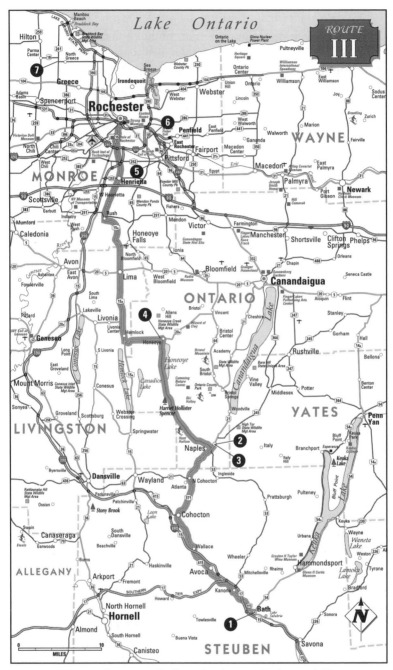

Route III. South to North from Bath via Naples and Honeoye to Rochester

# III. South to north from Bath via Naples and Honeoye to Rochester

This route went from Bath through Avoca, Wallace, and Cohocton to Naples and then along Honeoye Lake's West Lake Road and via Honeoye, Hemlock, Lima, Rush, Henrietta, and Brighton to Rochester.

1.  **Bath, 125 Washington Street**—The small two-story frame house on the south side of Washington Street was a station on the Underground Railroad that received refugee slaves from Elmira, Big Flats, and the Corning area. In emergencies, the slaves were hidden in a fruit cellar in the basement. From this station, escaped slaves were transported to Naples or to Penn Yan on their way north.

2.  **Naples, 1 Mechanic Street**—The two-story frame house with one-story additions on each side was once the home and funeral parlor of William (Uncle Billy) Marks, Jr., who transported slaves in his horse-drawn hearses. Sometimes the slaves were transported in coffins; the hearse had a trapdoor if the refugees had to get away in a hurry. Uncle Billy also ran a furniture store that was located next to his funeral parlor. The furniture store has been torn down and replaced by office buildings on Main Street. Uncle Billy hid the escaped slaves in the loft over his shop area. Loose planks were set aside to admit his visitors to the loft, where they slept on loose straw.

    The escaped slaves usually came to Uncle Billy's house at night via Naples Creek. He transported most of his charges to the Pitt Mansion at Honeoye, one of the next stops to the north on the Underground Railroad. Uncle Billy helped over 600 slaves escape to Canada.

3.  **Naples, 105 N. Main Street**—Built in 1841, the "Maxfield Inn" is a Greek Revival home that was in the Maxfield family for three generations. Hiram Maxfield established the first bank in Naples and one of the first wineries in town. The first floor of the inn includes a front and a rear parlor and an antique staircase leading to the second and third floors. The inn has one of the oldest private wine cellars in the area, which contains wine from the 1800s.

Maxfield Inn Carriage House, Naples

The carriage house behind the inn was a station on the Underground Railroad. A rock-lined tunnel used by fugitive slaves still exists below the carriage house. The tunnel connected the carriage house with a barn next door that has been torn down.

**4. Honeoye, Route 20A**—The "Pitt Homestead" is a two-story colonial house that was built in 1821 by Gideon Pitts, the son of Captain Peter Pitts—the first settler in the area around the village of Honeoye. Gideon Pitts, Jr., was a conductor on the Underground Railroad.

Escaped slaves hid in the basement in an unfinished cistern that never held water. The basement has five rooms, one of which is a walled-off room that may have contained the cistern. It is rumored that a tunnel used by the slaves ran from the basement to a barn behind the house. No signs of the tunnel are visible today.

Helen Pitts, the daughter of Gideon Pitts, Jr., was the second wife of Frederick Douglass, editor and abolitionist. The mixed marriage caused a stir in 1884. Douglass responded to critics with, "My first wife was the color of my mother, and my second wife was the color of my father." Helen's viewpoint was, "Love came to me, and I was not afraid to marry the man I loved because of his color."

**5. Pittsford, 52 South Main Street**—The "Hargous-Briggs House" is a stately brick two-story mansion with four chimneys built by Augustus Elliott for his fiancée, the daughter of Daniel Penfield— founder of the village of Penfield. It is rumored that she decided not to marry Elliott and never lived in the house. Judge Ashley Sampson, an ardent abolitionist, lived there in the 1820s and was a stationmaster on the Underground Railroad. A secret chamber in the basement used as a temporary hiding place for refugee slaves was a large, abandoned bake oven. A secret passage of narrow stairs between the south parlor rooms leads from the basement to the attic.

The house is named for Sally Hargous, a New York socialite, who lived in the house after Judge Sampson moved to Brooks Avenue, where he continued his Underground Railroad activities. The story that there was a large underground cavern under the village of Pittsford that was connected to the Hargous-Briggs House and other stations on the Underground Railroad has never been verified. If the tunnels ever did exist, they have been filled in and are not there

133

Hargous-Briggs House, Pittsford

today. The mansion is now used for the administrative offices of the St. Louis parish parochial school.

**6. Brighton, 1496 Clover Street**—was built in the 1820s by Isaac Moore, an ardent abolitionist who married a relative of William Clough Bloss, a leader in the abolitionist movement in Rochester. The stately, two-story brick house is called the Babcock House because three generations of the Babcock family lived there from the early 1860s until 1944.

In 1895, A. Emerson Babcock, supervisor of the town of Brighton for many years, installed modern plumbing in the house. The wooden basement stairs collapsed under the weight of the workmen and revealed a secret chamber. The room was eight feet wide by ten feet long and could accommodate twelve fugitives. It was rumored that the chamber led to a tunnel. Many chicken bones were found on the floor of the room, leading investigators to believe that escaped slaves hid there. The supervisor's son, William J. Babcock, recalled seeing the "drumsticks" in the cellar as a young man.

**7. Greece, 1191 Manitou Road**—a beautiful, two-story cobblestone house was built in the 1830s by Isaac Chase, a retired New England sea captain. The house, which is set back from Manitou Road, is not far from the shore of Lake Ontario. The home had a trap door over a wooden stairway that led to a secret room in the basement. Chase's son, Isaac, Jr. was active in the Underground Railroad during the 1840s and 1850s. He transported many slaves via wagon to Lake Ontario, where they boarded boats to take them to Canada.

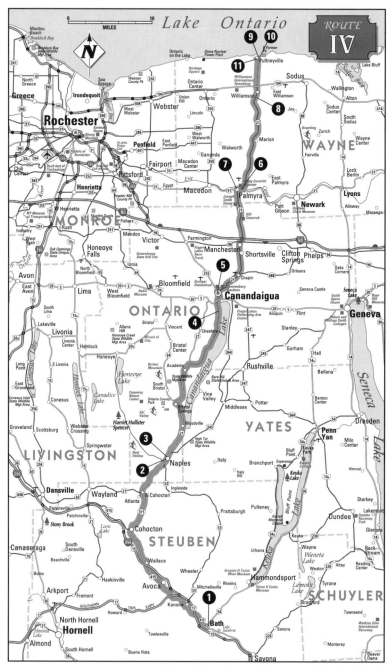

Route IV. South to North from Bath via Naples, Canandaigua, and Palmyra to Pultneyville

## IV. South to north from Bath via Naples, Canandaigua, and Palmyra to Pultneyville

Route IV proceeded north from Bath through Avoca, Wallace, and Cohocton to Naples and then along Canandaigua Lake's West Lake Road to Canandaigua. From this point, some of the refugees traveled northwest to Rochester and others went north via Shortsville, Manchester, Palmyra, Marion, and Williamson to Pultneyville.

1.  **Bath, 125 Washington Street**—The small two-story frame house on the south side of Washington Street was a station on the Underground Railroad that received refugee slaves from Elmira, Big Flats, and the Corning area. In emergencies, the slaves were hidden in a fruit cellar in the basement. From this station, escaped slaves were transported to Naples or to Penn Yan on their way north.

2.  **Naples, 1 Mechanic Street**—The two-story frame house with one-story additions on each side was once the home and funeral parlor of William ("Uncle Billy") Marks, Jr., who transported slaves in his horse-drawn hearses. Sometimes the slaves were transported in coffins; the hearse had a trapdoor if the refugees had to get away in a hurry. Uncle Billy also ran a furniture store that was located next to his funeral parlor. The furniture store has been torn down and replaced by office buildings on Main Street. Uncle Billy hid the escaped slaves in the loft over his shop area. Loose planks were set aside to admit his visitors to the loft, where they slept on loose straw.

    The escaped slaves usually came to Uncle Billy's house at night via Naples Creek. He transported most of his charges to the Pitt Mansion at Honeoye, one of the next stops to the north on the Underground Railroad. Uncle Billy helped over 600 slaves escape to Canada.

3.  **Naples, 105 N. Main Street**—Built in 1841, the "Maxfield Inn" is a Greek Revival home that was in the Maxfield family for three generations. Hiram Maxfield established the first bank in Naples and one of the first wineries in town. The first floor of the inn includes a front and a rear parlor and an antique staircase leading to the second and third floors. The inn has one of the oldest pri-

vate wine cellars in the area, which contains wine from the 1800s.

The carriage house behind the inn was a station on the Underground Railroad. A rock-lined tunnel used by fugitive slaves still exists below the carriage house. The tunnel connected the carriage house with a barn next door that has been torn down.

**4. Canandaigua, 3402 W. Lake Road—The "Cobblestone Farm"** was built by Isaac Parrish and after it was purchased by Robert and Maggie Gorham Benedict in 1858. Escaped slaves were transported to Cobblestone Farm from Naples by William ("Uncle Billy") Marks, Jr., in one of his mortuary's horse-drawn hearses.

The fugitives were hidden in a secret room in the attic adjacent to the south wall of Cobblestone Farm. They were led up to the attic where they walked on loose floorboards around the south chimney through a doorway into a small room, which was six feet wide and ten feet long. The ceiling was five feet, four inches high at the peak sloping down to four feet where the ceiling joined the walls. The back wall is stone and mortar, and the walls are plaster. The room would have been stifling hot in the summer—it had no windows—and bitter cold in the winter.

**5. Canandaigua, 104 Gibson Street—The** graceful two-story frame house with a mansard roof and detailed ornamental trim was a station on the Underground Railroad on routes both to Rochester and to Pultneyville. In emergencies, slaves descended through a trap door in the dining room to a dry cistern in the basement. The trap door was near the north wall of the dining room and was covered by the dining room table. Most of the escaped slaves arrived in Canandaigua either from Naples or from Geneva on their way to Canada.

**6. Palmyra, 322 E. Main Street—The** two-story brick house was built by Pliny Sexton, a Quaker jeweler, in the 1830s. Today, a historic marker in front of the home notes that it was used a station on the Underground Railroad. Sexton hid the refugee slaves under a load of hay or vegetables in his wagon and conveyed them to the next station on the Underground Railroad, enroute north to Pultneyville on the shore of Lake Ontario or northwest via Perinton to Rochester. Pliny Sexton, Jr., helped his father with the slaves; he became more well-known than his father as a banker, lawyer, and Chancellor of the New York State Board of Regents.

**7. Palmyra, 101 E. Main Street**—The Western Presbyterian Church, one of the churches on each of the four corners of Palmyra at the intersection of routes 21 and 31, was an active station on the Underground Railroad. Escaped slaves were hidden in the belfry of the church until they could be transported to the next station on the Underground Railroad on the way to Williamson and Pultneyville. They left the church at night via an underground tunnel that led northward toward the Erie Canal.

**8. Williamson, 5825 Route 21**—The three-story fieldstone house with its eighteen-inch-thick walls now covered with stucco was built in 1838 by Griffith Cooper, a Quaker and active abolitionist. It is located five miles south of Pultneyville. Fugitive slaves were hidden in a secret chamber in the attic. In the 1950s, David Oakleaf, whose parents owned the home at the time, found small doors on the east and west sides of the attic that were blocked by large boxes. Each door led to a triangular space formed by the roofline. David crawled along the passageway and found a chamber that could accommodate eight to ten people for short periods of time without much room to spare.

David's grandmother, Irilene Oakleaf, told him a story passed on to her by her great-grandfather, Griffith Cooper. Once slave-catchers came to the farmhouse looking for escaped slaves. Suspecting that escaped slaves had hidden in a pile of hay, they plunged their swords into it. They left without finding any refugees. In fact, several fugitives were hiding in the hay, and one of them had been stabbed and injured severely. However, he didn't cry out, and he didn't give away his presence and that of his friends.

**9. Pultneyville, 4184 Washington Street**—The "Captain Throop House" is a cobblestone house built in 1832 by Captain Horatio N. Throop. Samuel Cuyler was an associate of Captain Throop on the Underground Railroad. Cuyler's son, Ledyard, transported many wagonloads of fugitive slaves from Sodus and other Underground Railroad stations to his father's estate in the middle of the night. The Cuylers would take their passengers to Captain Throop and say, "I have some passengers for you." Captain Throop would respond, "My

Captain Throop House, Pultneyville

boat runs for passengers." One of the vessels that Captain Throop used to transport escaped slaves to Canada was the Steamer *Express*, which was owned by a partnership company. Captain Throop commanded this vessel from 1839 to 1842.

Captain Throop's brother, Captain Washington S. Throop, was also in the shipping business, but it is not certain whether he helped fugitive slaves. However, their nephew, James T. Holling, who was also a lake boat captain, was active in the Underground Railroad movement. One one occasion, he took some escaped slaves across Lake Ontario to Presque Isle, off the shoreline of Canada. The slaves were so relieved to have gained their freedom that they knelt in prayer.

**10. Pultneyville, 7851 Jay Street**—The "Selby House," a two-story, frame house with a one-story addition at the back, was built in 1808 by Jeremiah Selby. The piers directly across Washington street from the house were the point of departure for slaves being transported to Canada by ship. Escaped slaves were hidden temporarily behind the Selby home among large piles of wood while waiting to board Captain Throop's ship. During the War of 1812, one of the Royal Navy ships of Commodore Yeo's squadron fired two cannonballs through the front wall of the Selby House.

**11. Pultneyville, 4194 Washington Street**—The "Hasselwander House" is a beautiful, two-story, brick home with a cupola. It was one of the Pultneyville Underground Railroad stations. The slaves were hidden in a frame addition at the rear of the house.

In Pultneyville, escaped slaves boarded ships bound for Peterboro and other Ontario ports.

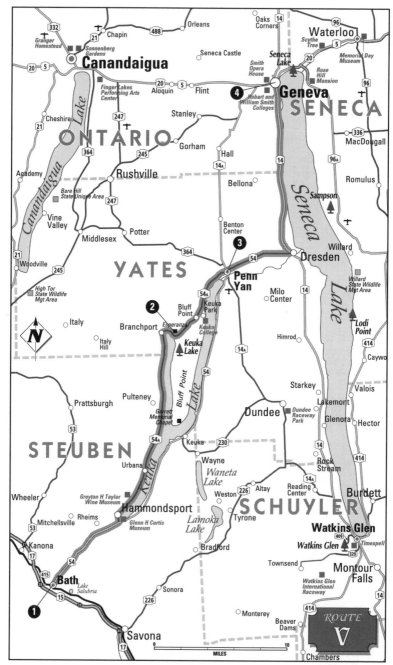

Route V. South to North from Bath via Branchport and Penn Yan
to Geneva and Routes 5 and 20

# V. South to north from Bath via Branchport and Penn Yan to Geneva and Routes 5 and 20

An alternate route went from Penn Yan through Middlesex and along the east side of Canandaigua Lake to Canandaigua and then either northwest to Rochester or north via Palmyra to Pultneyville.

**1. Bath, 125 Washington Street**—The small two-story frame house on the south side of Washington Street was a station on the Underground Railroad that received refugee slaves from Elmira, Big Flats, and the Corning area. In emergencies, the slaves were hidden in a fruit cellar in the basement. From this station, escaped slaves were transported to Naples or to Branchport and Penn Yan on their way north.

**2. Jerusalem, Route 54A near Branchport**—Esperanza is an impressive nineteen-room Greek Revival mansion with two-story Ionic columns and 6,000 square feet of space; it overlooks the bluff and the west branch of Keuka Lake from a hillside north of Route 54A and east of Branchport. Construction was completed on July 3, 1838, by its owner, John Nicholas Rose, who purchased over 1,000 acres of land in Yates County in 1823.

Rose had the mansion built as a wedding gift to his bride, and the name Esperanza was his adaptation of the Latin word for hope. He was the son of Robert Selden Rose and Jane Lawson Rose, who moved from Virginia to the site of the Rose Hill Mansion, near Geneva, in 1804. They brought their slaves with them, but freed them upon completion of their home overlooking the east shore of Seneca Lake.

Two and a half years were spent gathering stone for the cellar walls of Esperanza, which included boulders weighing up to 1,400 pounds. The walls are twenty-seven inches thick, the windows are six feet high, and there are seven fireplaces in the mansion—including one in the basement and two that are plastered over. A large bake-oven hearth in the kitchen is one of the two that are "hidden." Originally, an open staircase extended from the first floor near the entrance to the attic, which is networked with structural beams.

Esperanza is constructed of walls of stone with brick pilasters

Esperanza, near Branchport

covered with stucco. Sand for use in mixing the stucco was brought from the tip of Bluff Point, eight miles to the south, in Indian canoes. The weight-bearing interior partitions are solid masonry from the basement to the attic. The Ionic columns on the portico were made by enclosing large tree trunks in brick and then covering the brick with stucco.

The mansion has been the subject of a novel and the location for a movie. It has served as a private residence, a stop on the Underground Railroad, a sheep barn, the Yates County Home, an art gallery, and the Chateau Esperanza winery.

**3. Penn Yan, 129 Clinton Street**—The two-story frame house is located on the east side of Penn Yan on Route 54 from Dresden. Escaped slaves were transported from Bath to Penn Yan and then either to Geneva or Canandaigua on their way north.

**4. Geneva, 20 Pulteney Street**—The "Van Houten House" is a two-story, frame house with a one-story addition on its south side. When the house was remodeled years ago a bullet hole was found in the front door. Men chasing an escaped slaved fired the shot through the door. Just before they arrived, grandmother Van Houten, a spirited woman and a devout Methodist, heard shouting and saw an African-American running up the sidewalk toward the house. She let the escaped slave in and bolted the door. She gave him part of a loaf of bread, guided him out of the back door, and told him to rattle the back fence to let her know that he had escaped. She opened the door to the boisterous men and invited them to search her home. While they were searching the second floor, she heard the back fence being rattled.

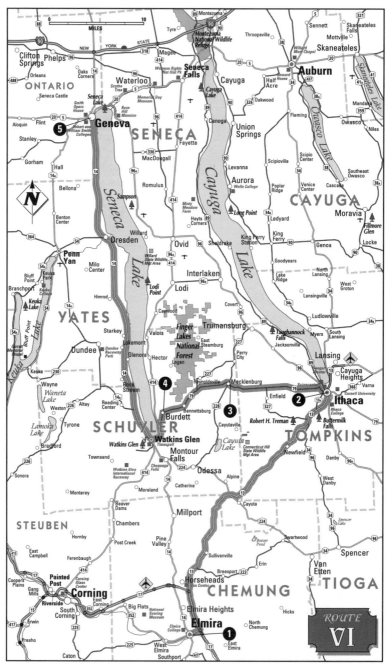

Route VI. South to North from Elmira via Ithaca and Watkins
Glen to Geneva and Routes 5 and 20

# VI. South to North from Elmira via Ithaca & Watkins Glen to Geneva and Routes 5 & 20

Another route from Elmira to Watkins Glen was through Big Flats, Corning, and Hornby. Millport and Montour Falls were on an alternate route. A principal station in Watkins Glen was Luther Cleveland's homestead north of the village at Gabriel's Junction, which was torn down to accommodate the redesign of the intersection of Routes 14 and 14A. The Underground Railroad route from Ithaca to Watkins Glen went through Mecklenburg and Burdett. In addition to the route along the west side of Seneca Lake through Dresden to Geneva, there was also a route along the east side of the lake via Lodi.

**1. Elmira, 311 Woodlawn Avenue**—The small one-story bungalow, which apparently is the only Underground Railroad station still standing in Elmira, was the home of John W. Jones, an ex-slave. The house, originally located on a sixteen-acre farm at 1259 College Avenue, was rotated ninety degrees when it was placed on a basement constructed for it at its present site. Jones, who was born into slavery in 1817 on a plantation in Leesburg, Virginia, escaped to the North in June, 1844.

In 1847, he was appointed sexton of the First Baptist Church in Elmira and in 1851 became an active stationmaster on the Underground Railroad. During his nine years as a stationmaster, he helped over 800 fugitive slaves to escape, usually in parties of six or seven. To his knowledge, none of them was caught. Elmira was a principal hub on the Underground Railroad. It received many slaves sent northward by William Still of Philadelphia.

**2. Ithaca, 116 Cleveland Avenue**—The St. James AME Zion Church was organized by Ithaca's African-American community in 1833 at the home of its first pastor, Reverend Henry Johnson. The two-story frame church with a two-level tower was built in 1836 on Wheat Street, later renamed Cleveland Avenue. The marker in front of the church notes, "It became the religious, political, and cultural-heart of the community and, in 1841, the site of a school for black children. It was home to Pastors Thomas James and Jermain Loguen

Parker Wixom Homestead, Mecklenburg

and host to Harriet Tubman and Frederick Douglass." The church was the site of many abolitionist meetings and was a station on the Underground Railroad between Elmira and Auburn / Syracuse.

**3. Mecklenburg, 4831 Buck Hill Road, near Carman Road—** The Parker Wixom homestead was one of several homes of Quaker families in the area that were stations on the Underground Railroad. Escaped slaves were hidden in a small room under the kitchen at the back of the house. The next station to the north was at Lodi in Seneca County.

**4. Burdett, 1780 Main Street—**The "John Ciprich House," a two-story frame home, is the oldest house in Burdett. The house was the station after Mecklenburg on the Underground Railroad when traveling west on the present Route 79 between Ithaca and Watkins Glen. Mary Pratt, who lived in the house in 1938, accidentally tore some wallpaper covering a fireplace. Escaped slaves had painted symbols in black paint on a cover over the fireplace opening. The letters B, T, and C accompanied drawings of a pointing hand, an African-American, a cross, shovels, a horse, and a bird in flight. The symbols were intended to represent the slave's flight as well as the Christian symbols of faith and hope.

**5. Geneva, 20 Pulteney Street—**The "Van Houten House" is a two-story frame house with a one-story addition on its south side. When the house was remodeled years ago a bullet hole was found in the front door. Men chasing an escaped slaved fired the shot through the door. Just before they arrived, grandmother Van Houten, a spirited woman and a devout Methodist, heard shouting and saw an African-American running up the sidewalk toward the house. She let the escaped slave in and bolted the door. She gave him part of a loaf of bread, guided him out of the back door, and told him to rattle the back fence to let her know that he had escaped. She opened the door to the boisterous men and invited them to search her home. While they were searching the second floor, she heard the back fence being rattled.

From Geneva, the escaped slaves traveled to Canandaigua and then either northwest to Rochester or north via Palmyra to Pultneyville.

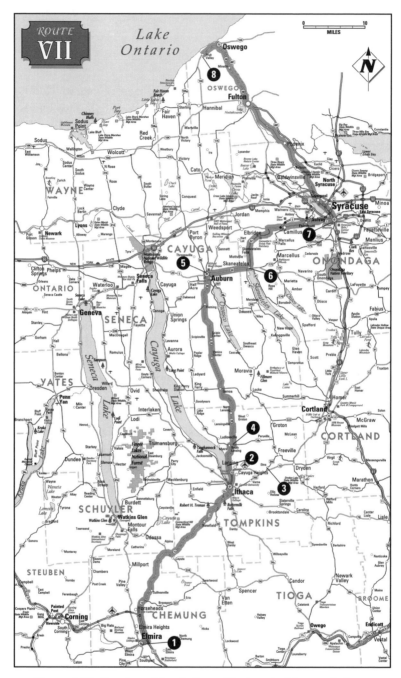

Route VII. South to North from Elmira via Ithaca, Auburn,
Skaneateles, and Syracuse to Oswego

150

# VII. SOUTH TO NORTH FROM ELMIRA VIA ITHACA, AUBURN, SKANEATELES, AND SYRACUSE TO OSWEGO

Another route north from Ithaca was by ship on the lake to Cayuga on the east shore and then across the Cayuga Bridge to Bridgeport and Seneca Falls and west. A wooden bridge spanned the northern end of Cayuga Lake from 1800 until 1853. A route proceeded north through Trumansburg and Interlaken along the west side of Cayuga Lake and another route followed the east side of the lake through Ludlowville.

From Auburn, fugitives had a choice of traveling west to Rochester or east to Syracuse and then north to Oswego. An alternate route from Ithaca to Auburn passed through Etna, Peruville, and Groton.

1. **Elmira, 311 Woodlawn Avenue**—The small one-story bungalow, which apparently is the only Underground Railroad station still standing in Elmira, was the home of John W. Jones, an ex-slave. The house, originally located on a sixteen-acre farm at 1259 College Avenue, was rotated ninety degrees when it was placed on a basement constructed for it at its present site. Jones, who was born into slavery in 1817 on a plantation in Leesburg, Virginia, escaped to the North in June 1844.

In 1847, he was appointed sexton of the First Baptist Church in Elmira and in 1851 became an active stationmaster on the Underground Railroad. During his nine years as a stationmaster, he helped over 800 fugitive slaves to escape, usually in parties of six or seven. To his knowledge, none of them was caught. Elmira was a principal hub on the Underground Railroad. It received many slaves sent northward by William Still of Philadelphia.

2. **Lansing, 1457 E. Shore Drive**—The "Greystone Inn" was built in 1838 and was a station on the Underground Railroad route along the east shore of Cayuga Lake to the village of Cayuga on the route north to Auburn. From Auburn the slaves were transported either east to Syracuse or west to Rochester and then across Lake Ontario to Canada. A second route went northeast through the town of

John W. Jones House, Elmira

Lansing to Auburn. Fugitive slaves were hidden in the attic and in the cupola of the Greystone Inn.

**3. Etna, 118 Lower Creek Road**—The historic marker in front of the Greek-revival frame farmhouse, which was built in 1844, bears the words "Underground Railroad—Home of William Hanford and wife Altha C. Todd, who sheltered fugitive slaves on way to Canada and freedom." A hidden trapdoor in the floor of the kitchen leads to a five feet wide by ten feet long "hidey hole" where the slaves hid from the slave-catchers. The hiding place was a false cistern that has no connection to gutters on the roof or to the downspouts.

**4. Lansing, Corner of Routes 34 and 34B**—"The Underground-Rogues' Harbor" is a three-story brick building built in 1830. It was initially called the Central Exchange Hotel, but was renamed Rogues' Harbor "for the many pirates and horse thieves who frequented the premises." It was named "The Underground" because of a tunnel that ran underneath the building, which was used by escaped slaves. The hotel was a station on the Underground Railroad route from Ithaca to Auburn.

**5. Auburn, 33 South Street**—The "Seward Mansion" was built in 1816-17 by Judge Elijah Miller, William H. Seward's father-in-law. The federal-style mansion, a registered National Historic Landmark, was expanded in 1847 and in 1860. All rooms in the 30-room house, half of which are open to the public, are furnished with original family pieces and gifts and memorabilia collected by Seward in his travels.

The parlor of Seward House contains the gilded furniture, upholstered with its original tapestry material, from the parlor of Seward's Washington home when he was Secretary of State in Abraham Lincoln's and Andrew Johnson's administrations. The fireplace mantel in the parlor was built by a sixteen-year-old journeyman painter and carpenter, Brigham Young, who inherited the leadership of the Mormon Church from its founder, Joseph Smith.

Guests who were served in the dining room included Presidents John Quincy Adams, Martin Van Buren, Andrew Johnson, and William McKinley. Other luminaries who dined there were Henry Clay, General Custer, Admiral Farragut, General Grant, and Daniel Webster.

153

Seward Mansion, Auburn

Fugitive slaves who stopped at Seward House on their journey to freedom stayed in one large room and one small room on the second floor in the back of the mansion. They entered and left via a stairway off a passageway leading to the courtyard just around the corner from the kitchen. The two beautiful stone outbuildings, or carriage houses, in back of the mansion were not used to hide escaped slaves. In the first half of the nineteenth century the property was an operating farm. One of the outbuildings was used as a stable and the other was used to store farm implements.

6.  **Skaneateles, 98 W. Genesee Street**—"Evergreen House" is the only documented Underground Railroad station still standing in Skaneateles. The house was built by James Canning Fuller, a Quaker who arrived in Skaneateles from England on April 20, 1834. Fuller was a strong abolitionist who gave many speeches on the subject. Mr. and Mrs. Fuller traveled to the South to buy slaves, whom they released when they arrived back in the North. The Reverend Jermain Wesley Loguen, who was active in the Underground Railroad movement in Syracuse, stayed with the Fullers for three or four days enroute to escaping to Canada.

After his death on November 25, 1847, Fuller's widow continued to use the house as an Underground Railroad station. Their son was an active member of the Anti-Slavery Society in Syracuse. Mrs. Fuller sold the home to James A. Root, an abolitionist who continued to operate the house as a stop on the Underground Railroad.

The T-shaped Evergreen House has three columns and a porch and second-story veranda at its eastern entrance. No hiding places used by escaped slaves have been found in the house.

7.  **Syracuse, 304 E. Onondaga Street (overlooking Columbus Circle)**—The Wesleyan Methodist Church is one of the last remaining Underground Railroad stations in Syracuse. In a one-month period in the early 1850s, church member Luther Lee helped thirty-four fugitive slaves to escape. The church is also one of the few survivors of the many Syracuse churches and buildings where abolitionist meetings were held. The Wesleyan Methodist Church broke from the Methodist Church in the early 1840s over the issue of slavery. Construction of the red brick church was completed in 1846. The brick tower at the west entrance and the two-story structure at the

Wesleyan Methodist Church, Columbus Circle, Syracuse

east side of the church were completed in 1858. In 1878, a spire was added to the tower.

Seven sculptures have been carved into clay in the wall in the fifty-foot-long basement of the church. It is believed that they were carved by fugitive slaves who were hiding in the church on their route to Canada and freedom. Only one of the seven unfired-clay faces remains in its original form without substantial deterioration; however, the nose on the face is chipped. The hair is parted on one side in page style, and there are no pupils in the almond-shaped eyes. A member of an archaeological team from Syracuse University interprets the face as a composite of two people—abolitionist leaders Frederick Douglass, who spoke in the church, and the Reverend Jermain Loguen of Syracuse.

Dating by archaelogists of Underground Railroad activity is based on a fragment found in the basement cavern of a black-transfer print dish, which was a style of whiteware used from 1830 to 1850. The church is listed in the National Register of Historic Places.

**8. Fruit Valley (Oswego County), 4661 Cemetery Road**—The two-story Federal-style frame house was built between 1816 and 1826 by Daniel Pease and Miriam Rice Pease. The New York State Historical Society marker in the front yard comments "Site of Underground [Railroad] Station—Edwards Residence 1860-65—Slaves Transferred From Here to 'Old Homestead.'" The farmhouse was an important stop on the Auburn-Oswego route of the Underground Railroad. Two generations of Peases, Daniel and Miriam and their seven children, were stationmasters. They hid the slaves in a woodshed at the rear of the house. From there, they were transported to the piers in Oswego to board a ship to Canada.

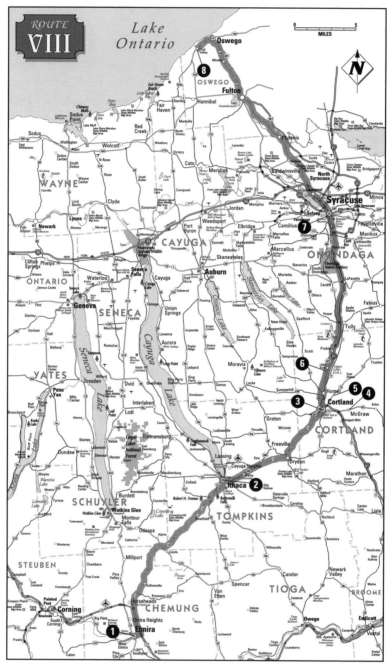

Route VIII. South to North from Elmira via Ithaca, Cortland, and
Syracuse to Oswego

# VIII. SOUTH TO NORTH FROM ELMIRA VIA ITHACA, CORTLAND, AND SYRACUSE TO OSWEGO

From Cortland, the fugitives traveled through Homer, Little York, Tully, and LaFayette on their journey to Syracuse.

**1. Elmira, 311 Woodlawn Avenue**—The small one-story bunga-low, which is apparently the only Underground Railroad station still standing in Elmira, was the home of John W. Jones, an ex-slave. The house, originally located on a sixteen-acre farm at 1259 College Avenue, was rotated ninety degrees when it was placed on a base-ment constructed for it at its present site. Jones, who was born into slavery in 1817 on a plantation in Leesburg, Virginia, escaped to the North in June 1844.

In 1847, he was appointed sexton of the First Baptist Church in Elmira and in 1851 became an active stationmaster on the Underground Railroad. During his nine years as a stationmaster, he helped over 800 fugitive slaves to escape, usually in parties of six or seven. To his knowledge, none of them was caught. Elmira was a principal hub on the Underground Railroad. It received many slaves sent northward by William Still of Philadelphia.

**2. Ithaca, 116 Cleveland Avenue**—The St. James AME Zion Church was organized by Ithaca's African-American community in 1833 at the home of its first pastor, Reverend Henry Johnson. The two-story frame church with a two-level tower was built in 1836 on Wheat Street, later renamed Cleveland Avenue. The marker in front of the church notes, "It became the religious, political, and cultural heart of the community and, in 1841, the site of a school for black children. It was home to Pastors Thomas James and Jermain Loguen and host to Harriet Tubman and Frederick Douglass." The church was the site of many abolitionist meetings and was a station on the Underground Railroad between Elmira and Auburn / Syracuse.

**3. Cortland, 96-98 Port Watson Street**—The two-story frame building has housed the Calvary Bible Church, the Calvary Baptist Church, and the First Baptist Church. The roofline has been modi-fied considerably from its original configuration. The church was an

St. James AME Zion Church, Ithaca

important station on the Underground Railroad prior to the Civil War. The basement of the church was connected to the Judd Stevens homestead at 94 Port Watson Street by a quarter-mile-long tunnel. Harriet Tubman used this station as a rest stop for some of the 300 slaves she guided to freedom.

**4. McGraw, 21-19 W. Academy Street**—The large two-story frame house built by Israel Palmer using hand-hewn beams has been converted to a double house. A 1,700-foot-long tunnel was constructed from the basement of the home to the bank of Smith Creek, which empties into McGraw Creek. A secret door with a frame on a pivot was built into the wall of the basement. The sides of the door were left jagged to help to conceal it. Entered by pushing on the door and stepping down five stairs, the tunnel was lined with large, heavy stones held together with "dry masonry." A person of average height had to stoop to walk trough the tunnel, which was only two feet wide.

The tunnel entrance has been cemented shut in the basement, and the exit on the creek bank was sealed during the 1930s when the WPA constucted riprap walls along the creekbank. Herman Doran, a baker from Homer, verified the existence of the tunnel. In his youth, he walked the entire length of the tunnel from the basement of the farmhouse to Smith Creek.

**5. Cortland, 1739 Clinton Street**—The "Cooper Farmhouse" is a two-story frame home, later owned by the Van Schaick family. The farmhouse was a station on the Underground Railroad between Cortland and Syracuse. An alternate route was from this station to the Smith farm in Peterboro, a staging point, and then to Syracuse.

**6. Little York, Corner of Route 281 and Cold Brook Road**—The two-story frame home, which was built by Oren Cravath, has an historic marker in the front yard bearing the words "Salisbury-Pratt Homestead—used before the Civil War as an 'underground railroad station' where Oren Cravath sheltered & aided fugitive slaves on their way to Canada." The home was a station on the Underground Railroad route between Cortland and Syracuse.

**7. Syracuse, 304 E. Onondaga Street (overlooking Columbus**

Salisbury-Pratt Homestead, Little York

Circle)—The Wesleyan Methodist Church is one of the last remaining Underground Railroad stations in Syracuse. In a one-month period in the early 1850s, church member Luther Lee helped thirty-four fugitive slaves to escape. The church is also one of the few survivors of the many Syracuse churches and buildings where abolitionist meetings were held. The Wesleyan Methodist Church broke from the Methodist Church in the early 1840s over the issue of slavery. Construction of the red brick church was completed in 1846. The brick tower at the west entrance and the two-story structure at the east side of the church were completed in 1858. In 1878, a spire was added to the tower.

Seven sculptures have been carved into clay in the wall of the fifty-foot-long basement of the church. It is believed that they were carved by fugitive slaves who were hidden in the church on their route to Canada and freedom. Only one of the seven unfired-clay faces remains in its original form without substantial deterioration; however, the nose on the face is chipped. The hair is parted on one side in page style, and there are no pupils in the almond-shaped eyes. A member of an archaeological team from Syracuse University interprets the face as a composite of two people—abolitionist leaders Frederick Douglass, who spoke in the church, and the Reverend Jermain Loguen of Syracuse.

Dating by archaelogists of Underground Railroad activity is based on a fragment found in the basement cavern of a black-transfer print dish, which was a style of whiteware used from 1830 to 1850. The church is listed in the National Register of Historic Places.

**8. Fruit Valley (Oswego County), 4661 Cemetery Road**—The two-story Federal-style frame house was built between 1816 and 1826 by Daniel Pease and Miriam Rice Pease. The New York State Historical Society marker in the front yard comments "Site of Underground [Railroad] Station—Edwards Residence 1860-65—Slaves Transferred From Here to 'Old Homestead.'" The farmhouse was an important stop on the Syracuse-Oswego route of the Underground Railroad. Two generations of Peases, Daniel and Miriam and their seven children, were stationmasters. They hid the slaves in a woodshed at the rear of the house. From there, they were transported to the piers in Oswego to board a ship to Kingston, Ontario.

The village of Phoenix was an intermediate stop on the

Underground Railroad between Syracuse and Oswego. Other stations were located in the village of Mexico to the east of Oswego.

# Epilogue

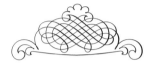

*"When that chariot comes, I'm going to leave you.*

*I'm bound for the promised land, friends, I'm going to leave you.*

*I'm sorry friends, to leave you, farewell! Oh farewell!*

*But I'll meet you in the morning, farewell! Oh farewell!*

*I'll meet you in the morning, when I reach the promised land;*

*On the other side of Jordan, for I'm bound for the promised land."*

—*Spiritual*

Many abolitionists and agents of the Underground Railroad experienced imprisonment, injury, and death. Calvin Fairbanks of Ohio spent over seventeen years in the Kentucky penitentiary for helping slaves to escape. Abolitionist editor William Lloyd Garrison escaped out of a back window when a Boston mob invaded the hall in which he was scheduled to speak. The mob attempted to throw him out of a second-story window, his clothes were half ripped from his body, and he was pulled through the streets by a rope tied around his waist.

For protection, he was lodged overnight in a jail. On the wall of his cell, he wrote, "William Lloyd Garrison was put into this cell on October 21, 1835, to save him from the violence of a respectable and influential mob who sought to destroy him for preaching the abominal and dangerous doctrine that all men are created equal, and that all oppression is odious in the sight of God."

Thomas Garrett, the leader of the Underground Railroad in Wilmington, was stripped of all his worldly possessions by a Delaware court for aiding refugee slaves. He responded, "Friend, I haven't a dollar in the world, but if thee knows a fugitive anywhere on the face of the earth who needs a breakfast, send him to me."

Levi Coffin, the president of the Underground Railroad in Cincinnati, became the object of verbal abuse, was physically attacked, and lived with threats to burn down his house and his business. On one occasion, proslavery activists threatened to set fire to the entire town in which he lived.

Richard Dillingham of Oberlin, Ohio, died in the Kentucky penitentiary where he was confined for helping runaway slaves. Seth Concklin, an agent of the Underground Railroad in Philadelphia, "was found drowned, with his hands and feet in chains and his skull fractured" while attempting to lead escaped slaves to freedom. Elijah Lovejoy, the editor of the abolitionist journal, *The Observer*, was shot and killed in Alton, Illinois, while attempting to save his press from destruction by a mob.

The brave men and women who helped their fellow human beings escape from bondage deserve all of the praise that we can give them. They acted in the way dictated by their consciences, rather than following the immoral and unjust laws that existed at the time. They were willing to endure imprisonment, injury, and even death for a cause that they knew was just.

However, the true heroes and heroines in this drama were the escaping slaves themselves. They were the real risk-takers. If captured, they were subject to beatings and to "being sold south," that is, being sent to a deep-south slave state where life was even more difficult. They ran away even if it meant the break-up of the family. They attempted to be reunited with their families, but, in many cases, they never saw their mothers, fathers, wives, husbands, sisters, brothers, daughters, or sons again.

They left the plantations with little more than the clothes on their backs, a little food, and directions to follow the North Star. When they sought food and shelter along the way north, they were never sure whether the people who opened the door on which they knocked would be friendly. The journey was tiring and the weaker travelers worried about slowing down the others and exposing them to increased risk.

The hardiest members of the slave community—either physically stronger, more strong-willed, or both—were usually the ones who undertook the risks of running away from the plantations. Those who escaped are the ones who really deserve our acclaim. They demonstrated strong human qualities.

Many of the descendants of these individuals have distinguished themselves in society, particularly in the fields of entertainment, sports, and the military, but also in education, the law, medicine, science, and many other fields. In music, not only have they made notable achievements in popular music, opera, and religious music, they have created new forms of music, such as jazz and its many variations.

When a spokesman was needed to speak out against civil injustices, they produced him. Martin Luther King employed the passive resistance methods of Mahatma Gandhi to spearhead the Civil Rights Movement. It took longer than anyone imagined, and there are still gains to be achieved, but significant accomplishments have been made. We can all learn from the enslaved who risked all to be free and the men and women who were willing to break the law to help them, despite the threat of physical injury and economic ruin.

# Follow the Drinking Gourd
[The Big Dipper and the North Star]

*Chorus:*
Follow the drinking gourd!
Follow the drinking gourd.
For the old man is awaiting
for to carry you to freedom
If you follow the drinking gourd.
When the sun comes back,
and the first quail calls,
Follow the drinking gourd.
For the old man is awaiting
for to carry you to freedom
If you follow the drinking gourd.

*(Repeat chorus)*
The riverbank makes a very good road,
The dead trees will show you the way.
Left foot, peg foot, traveling on,
Follow the drinking gourd.

*(Repeat chorus)*
When the great big river meets the little river,
Follow the drinking gourd.
For the old man is a-waiting for to carry you to freedom
If you follow the drinking gourd.

*(Repeat chorus)*
The river ends between two hills,
Follow the drinking gourd.
There's another river on the other side,
Follow the drinking gourd.

—— Underground Railroad Song

# Bibliography

Armstrong, Douglas and Louann Wurst. "Underground Railway Site at Syracuse's Wesleyan Methodist Church." Syracuse: Onondaga Historical Association, 1994.

Bearse, Austin. *Reminiscences of a Fugitive – Slave Law Days.* Boston: Warren Richardson, 1880.

Bentley, Judith. *Harriet Tubman.* New York: Franklin Watts, 1990.

Blockson, Charles L. *The Underground Railroad.* New York: Berkley Books, 1989.

Bontemps, Arna, ed. *Great Slave Narratives.* Boston: Beacon Press, 1969.

Breitbeck, Helen. "Trail to Freedom: The Underground Railroad and Abolitionist Movement in Oswego County." Oswego: White Marine Museum, n.d.

Breyfogle, William. *Make Free: The Story of the Underground Railroad.* Philadelphia: Lippincott, 1958.

Brown, John, ed. "UGRR Unlimited: The Alleluiah Freedom Road." *Yesteryears* 40 (June 1967): 169-79.

Buckmaster, Henrietta. *Flight to Freedom: The Story of the Underground Railroad.* New York: Thomas Y. Crowell, 1958.

Campbell, Stanley W. *The Slave Catchers, Enforcement of the Fugitive Slave Law 1850-60.* Chapel Hill: U of North Carolina P, 1968.

*Chemung Historical Journal.* "Underground Railroad: Route to Freedom." (June, 1961): 860-865.

Coffin, Levi. *Reminiscences of Levi Coffin.* Cincinnati: n.p.,1876 .

Cosner, Shaaron. *The Underground Railroad.* New York: Franklin Watts, 1991.

Davis, Charles T. and Henry Louis Gates, Jr., eds. *The Slave's Narrative.* New York: Oxford UP, 1985.

Douglass, Frederick. *Life and Times of Frederick Douglass.* New York: Thomas Y. Crowell, 1966.

Fairbanks, Calvin. *Rev. Calvin Fairbanks During Slavery Times.* Chicago: Patriotic Publishing, 1890.

Gadua, Renee K. "Time Shrouds Underground Railroad." *Syracuse Herald-American.* 28 Feb. 1995: C 2.

Gallwey, Sydney H. "Underground Railroad in Tompkins County." Ithaca: DeWitt Historical Society, 1963.

Gara, Larry. *The Liberty Line: The Legend of the Underground Railroad.* Lexington: U of Kentucky P, 1967.

Harlow, Ralph Volney. *Gerrit Smith: Philanthropist and Reformer.* New York: Henry Holt, 1939.

Haskins, James. *Get On Board: The Story of the Underground Railroad.* New York: Scholastic, 1993.

Holland, Frederic. *Frederick Douglass: The Colored Orator. New York: Funk & Wagnalls,* 1895.

Huggins, Nathan Irvin. *Slave and Citizen: The Life of Frederick Douglass.* Boston: Little, Brown, 1980.

Hunter, Carol M. *To Set the Captives Free: Reverend Jermain Wesley Loguen and the Struggle for Freedom in Central New York 1835-1872.* New York: Garland, 1993.

Kanestio Historical Society. "Older Homes of Canisteo." Canisteo, New York, 1989.

Khan, Lurey. *One Day, Levin ... He Be Free: William Still and the Underground Railroad.* New York: Dutton, 1972.

Klees, Emerson. *People of the Finger Lakes Region: The Heart of New York State.* Rochester: Friends of the Finger Lakes Publishing, 1995.

McGowan, James A. *Station Master on the Underground Railroad: The Life and Letters of Thomas Garrett.* Moylan, Pennsylvania: Whimsie Press, 1977.

McClard, Megan. *Harriet Tubman: Slavery and the Underground Railroad.* Englewood Cliffs, New Jersey: Silver Burdett, 1991.

McDonough. Jill. "Elmira's Underground Route to Freedom." *Chemung Historical Journal.* (Sept. 1974): 2421-2427.

Mars, James. *Life of James Mars: A Slave Born and Sold in Connecticut.* Hartford: Case, Lockwood, 1865.

Merrill, Arch. *The Underground, Freedom's Road and Other Upstate Tales.* New York: American Book-Stratford, 1963.

Miller, Douglas T. *Frederick Douglass and the Fight for Freedom.* New York: Facts on File, 1988.

Mitchell, William M. *The Underground Railroad.* London: W. Tweedie, 1860.

Mutunhu, Tendai. *Afro-Americans in New York Life and History.* "Tompkins County: An Underground Railroad Transit in Central New York." Buffalo: Afro-American Historical Association of the Niagara Frontier, 3.2, July 1979: 15-33.

Nichols, Charles H. *Black Men in Chains: Narratives by Escaped Slaves*. New York: Lawrence Hill, 1972.

O'Connor, John. "The Jerry Incident and the Underground Railway." *Fifteenth Publication of the Oswego Historical Society*. Oswego: Palladium-Times, 1952.

Petit, Eber M. *Sketches in the History of the Underground Railroad*. Fredonia, New York: McKinstry & Son, 1879.

Phelan, Helene C. *And Why Not Everyman? An Account of Slavery, the Underground Railroad, and the Road to Freedom in New York's Southern Tier*. Almond, New York: privately printed, 1987.

Rapp, Marvin A. *Canal Water and Whiskey*. New York: Twayne, 1965.

Rappaport, Doreen. *Escape from Slavery: Five Journeys to Freedom*. New York: HarperCollins, 1991.

Richards, Karen M. "The Underground Railroad in Skaneateles." Skaneateles: Skaneateles Historical Society, n.d.

Roper, Moses. *A Narrative of the Adventures and Escape of Moses Roper from American Slavery*. New York: Negro Universities Press, 1970.

Ross, Alexander M. *Recollections and Experiences of an Abolitionist*. Toronto: Rowell and Hutchison, 1875.

Siebert, Wilbur H. *The Underground Railroad from Slavery to Freedom*. New York: Macmillan,1898.

Smedley, R.C. *History of the Underground Railroad*. Lancaster: Office of the *Journal*, 1883.

Still, William. *The Underground Rail Road*. Philadelphia: Porter & Coates,1872.

Strother, Horatio T. *The Underground Railroad in Connecticut*. Middletown, Connecticut: Wesleyan UP, 1962.

Taylor, M.W. *Harriet Tubman*. New York: Chelsea House, 1991.

Wright, Abner C. "Underground Railroad Activities in Elmira." *Chemung Historical Journal*. (Sept. 1968): 1754-58.

McBurney House, Canisteo

# Index

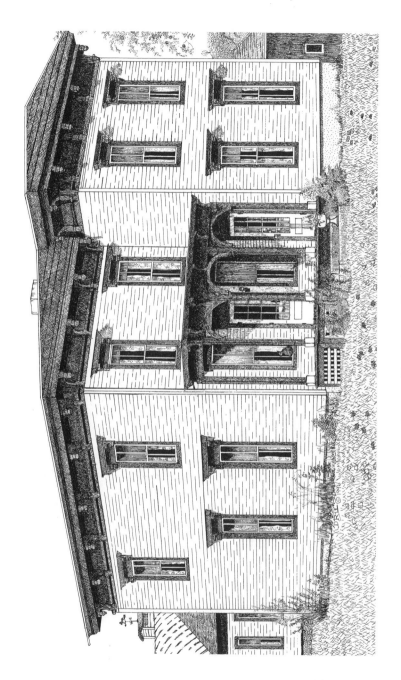

Cooper Farmhouse, Cortland